Copyright © 2022 by Shashi A.
All rights reserved. This book or any portion thereof
may not be reproduced or used in any manner whatsoever
without the express written permission of the publisher
except for the use of brief quotations in a book review.
Printed in the United States of America
Black Pearl Diamonds Publishing LLC, 2022
ISBN **9798366348225**
Black Pearl Diamonds Publishing LLC
Tulsa, OK 74112

BlackPearlDiamonds.com/Literary

mailto:info@blackpearldiamonds.com

TO
DEWAN CHAND ANAND

TABLE OF CONTENTS

§ * – PERSONAL ISSUES 2

§ * – FEEDING DESIRE 14

§ * – IN THE SWING OF THINGS 26

§ * – MARYANN 30

§ * – DOING BETTER BY HEART 39

§ * - TRAVELING 51

§ * – DID I? 62

§ * – WHICH TAB IS OPEN IN MY MIND 76

§ * – CAN'T BE YOUR SUPPLY 90

§ * – RECOGNITION MATTERS 100

Preface

In our life, at any age, going to a doctor's office for one reason or the other becomes unavoidable.

This book is written to bring to light as to what goes on behind the closed window. It is a lighthearted expression of how different personalities come together to make a team. It is like a family under one roof even though each in member is poles apart from the other one. They are put together in an environment where they must work together every day.

This book depicts many strange but true facts of life. The strangers becoming each other's best friends and support since it happens often. Sometimes the personalities clash which adds humor to this book.

Dr. Shashi A. Husain

§ * – PERSONAL ISSUES

That will be $6.20. When I heard that I came out of my room and went to the front office. I saw a lady by the name of India McDonough counting money for her copay. I went back to my office feeling embarrassed and somewhat ashamed. I never thought that I went to medical school to collect money from people for my services.

The year was 1982 and on January 2nd I opened my office for the first time. I had full support from several doctors introduced to me by Hillcrest Administration. I will forever remain indebted to them for getting me started on this life journey which is still going on.

My office assistant was Sue who had experience working for other doctors. She told me that she was 49 years old, single and in a relationship with a Surgeon. She looked like a mature woman who was neatly dressed and was easy to communicate with. She and I became very friendly and soon started sharing information about our families.

Later she told me that she had a daughter who was just playing with her husband and sending him a divorce decree to scare him. In a few weeks her 45 yrs. old daughter was divorced and that was very depressing to her. Sue was 69 years of age. She was nice to get me started but because she had a boyfriend who was also a physician, she did not seem very thrilled to do this job. She wanted time off to go on vacations frequently which was not possible because there was only one person working in the office. She started interviewing and helped me find Michelle as her replacement. Michelle was young, good looking without much experience but eager to work. She was trained for a few days and then was left to manage the office without any supervision. I had worked only as a teacher at New York medical College which is poles apart from being in private practice. I spoke to a few friends who gave me some helpful suggestions.

Michelle was a quick learner, soft spoken, very polite and a people pleaser. I was however taken aback by the way she dressed. Those days the females who worked in doctors' offices did not wear any kind of uniform. Soon I noticed that she only had two outfits. One of them was black satin pants and taffeta white shirt with big bell sleeves. The other one was long multi-layered freely white dress which looked more like a wedding dress. Fortunately, she did have a light but long jacket that she wore on top of her outfits every day. Most of the patients could only see the jacket as they will talk to her across the window. She wore eyeglasses with black frame and looked rather attractive.

Initially I did not notice her outfits because of the jacket she wore. Then it became apparent that she wore the same two outfits, which were not appropriate for the office, throughout the week. I finally had the courage to request her to dress professionally. She did not object to it and bought two pairs of scrubs which were appropriate for the office. By this time, she had already received her first paycheck.

Everything was going smoothly in the office for next 3 months. One morning while I was rounding at the hospital, I was called by the building manager that I should come to the office immediately as there was some fighting going on in my office. I rushed to my office and found front office in a topsy-turvy state. There were papers everywhere on the floor, the chairs were broken, and the front door handles were gone.

Couple of policemen were waiting for me. I was told that Michelle's boyfriend came to the office and beat her up badly. He also had an assault weapon in his hands. This was witnessed by the building manager. He ran out and called the police. They both were arrested for their behavior and because of their checkered past as per the information given to me by the officer who was waiting for me. It was apparent that I hardly knew her. On her application the address she wrote was not right and the name of the person that she gave for reference would not answer. I knew that she did not have a telephone. I was never informed by the police as to what happened to "' Michelle" if indeed that was her name

I called a few doctor's offices who I had met in the hospitals and asked how to get an emergency help for the office. I was referred to a staffing service. They sent a lady by the name of Linda. She was an EEG technician who also had experience working in doctor's offices She was a change from the previous two ladies who had worked for me. She was very pleasant, intelligent easy to talk to and had experience. Since I only had one person working for the office, she was supposed to do everything including the billing. She had plenty of time as we were only seeing 2-3 patients a day. She knew different insurance companies and the details about billing.

I thought I had hit a jackpot when Linda joined the front office. I had no complaints. I was not even worried about the money. I was told that doctors start collecting money about three months after they have seen patients. This was only five weeks since I opened the office. I was handwriting all notes so there was no typing involved. It was not very busy. I would be usually done by 1pm and then I would go and see new patients in the hospital. I was used to having residents and students with me while I was teaching but now, I had to go to three different hospitals to see one patient in each of them. It took several hours to finish the inpatient consults.

Sometimes I would be done early in the office or if the patient's canceled then I would have some free time. I would sometimes go to Utica square shops foe 15-20 minutes. I would feel on top of the world as it did not happen very often. Three months went by and there was hardly any money coming. I had borrowed $13,000 from the bank. I bought furniture for the office & an EMG machine. I was only able to pay Linda & meet the office expenses.

As I thought things were going smoothly it occurred to me, I should start getting some money from the insurance companies that we were billing. I did not even know how the process worked and who I could call to find out as to what was happening. I had exhausted the borrowed money. So now I was dipping into my savings to meet the expenses. Occasionally I would collect a few thousand dollars which kept me going. I was determined to continue as I had started liking what I was doing.

One day I got a letter from OU Medical Center offering me a teaching position in the Department of Neurology for which I had applied before moving to Oklahoma. This position was in Oklahoma City. Obviously, I could not move as my husband had already started his practice and was trying to get settled. So, I did not accept that position. However later I was given the position of an instructor in neurology at Oklahoma University Medical Center in Tulsa. They put me on teaching schedule. I would have medical students for rotation every month and had lecturers scheduled every so often. Teaching has always been my passion. I started enjoying my professional life a lot and did not care much about the happenings in the office. In other words, I was getting comfortable with the change in my professional life and started to get used to Private Practice. Linda used to do EEGS for the hospital prior to joining me. She encouraged me to buy an EEG machine so we could do the procedure in the office. Linda was able to handle all the activities in the office as we were not very busy.

I found her sitting at her desk looking very sad and crying one morning when I walked in. I asked her as to what had happened. Initially she was hesitant but later that day she informed me that she had been dating a physician for about 6 months. The relationship was not going right as he was trying to go back to his ex-wife. Since he would not talk to her on the phone, Linda started to write letters to him. Soon she found out that he was not responding to her letters either. Linda was divorced and did not have any children. This made the whole office situation very morose and sad. I soon realized I would have to find another person to work for us in the office as we were getting busy, and Linda was not able to handle her job. She was also responsible for billing which was not being done in a timely. By this time, I was pregnant with my second child. Unfortunately, I became very sick very early in the pregnancy and had to be hospitalized multiple times because of asthma. Linda was left alone in the office and had to reschedule patients every time I had a medical problem. Replacing Linda was out of question as I was too involved with my personal issues.

I had always wanted to relocate to Hillcrest Physicians building but there was no office space available. In late 1983 the only neurologist at hillcrest hospital decided to move back to New Zeeland. I was informed by Hillcrest Administration that I could have his office but not his patients. It was very exciting and thrilling to me. In November of 1983 I moved to suite number 520 in south physicians building which I am still occupying after 39 years. It was remodeled to my specifications which was very gratifying to me.

I bought new furniture, few cabinets and some paintings for the walls. I was very happy to have a decent-looking office. I had an open house and invited a few friends to come over. I hardly knew any doctors who could be invited for this event. One of my friends brought a money plant as a gift which I still have, and I cherish it. Moving to this building was a blessing. I could walk to the hospital several times a day and finish my work. I also started reading EEG'S for the hospital. I became acquainted with several other Physicians at the hospital. Within a few months another adult neurologist and a pediatric neurologist joined Hillcrest hospital and we became a group. We would share weekend calls while continuing office practice. It was very convenient.

On one side I was busy in my practice but at the same time I was getting sick every day. I was under the care of a pulmonologist for exacerbation of bronchial asthma. I continued to work as much as I could but had to take time off when my breathing would get bad.

Sometimes I would work all day and, in the evening, go home exhausted and drained. At night I would wake up several times because I could not breathe and had to use a machine to dilate my bronchi. This was taking toll on my practice.

Linda became frustrated quite often as she had to reschedule patients several times. She started telling the patients to find different neurologist behind my back. The practice was very slow not because I did not have any referrals. It was mainly because of my difficult pregnancy. I did not know what Linda was doing in my absence. She asked me to buy a fancy typewriter for her which also had memory. We did not have any computers at that time. This fancy typewriter became the biggest deal in my practice. It costed more than a laptop at this time. The secretary could type, store the documents and print them very efficiently. I was dictating office notes on a Dictaphone and then would give it to Linda to transcribe. It was perhaps too much for one person to handle even though we were still not very busy.

I knew things were not going smoothly in the office because I was sick and missing work very frequently. I was not well physically to supervise Linda. I had to be hospitalized several times. As soon as I would be out of the hospital I would start working full-time again. At home at night, I had to be on breathing treatments every 4 hours. The only way I could keep my sanity was to come to work.

My last day of work was June 5th, 1984. I had my son on June 7th. I took exactly four weeks off. There was another Neurologist by the name of Doctor Walker who covered for me. There were no patients seen for four weeks. The office was open every day and I would speak to Linda daily and take care of the office affairs from home. Dr. Walker was guidance to take pressure off Linda.

I came back to work with in four weeks after delivery. Linda oversaw all office affairs which was not running smoothly. I found out later, she was referring patients to other neurologists as she didn't want to be busy. I still had plenty of work to do. After a few weeks I hired Bonita. She looked very young and innocent. She lied on her resume saying that she was 18 years old while she was only 16 years of age. She was an islander and had difficulty pronouncing certain words. She was hard-working, keen to learn and not afraid to type or do some billing under Linda's guidance It took the pressure off Linda. She treated Bonita very well and trained her to handle several things such as medical terminology, filing, billing and answering the phone professionally. Bonita later informed me that Linda would often be crying after speaking to her boyfriend over the phone and leave the office for a while.

There was not enough money coming and the paperwork was mounting. Bonita could not finish the jobs assigned to her as she was still requiring lot of supervision which Linda could not always provide.

I started looking for somebody who would just do billing for us but could not find anyone.

I was astonished to find that Linda was just a fixture in the office. She was not doing anything excepting EEGS and some typing. Her demeanor was that of a depressed person. When I spoke to her about this, she informed me that she did not want to do any office work but would still be willing to do EEGS.

Within couple of weeks a friend referred a very nice lady by the name of Candice to me. She had experience and had a very pleasant personality. Everybody in the office liked that. She was a leader, a teacher and very professional. I could not have asked for a better office manager at that time. She was always on time and had many other skills besides the office work. I did have an accountant at the time but since Candice knew how to take out the taxes etc. soon, she started taking care of the pay roll every two weeks. I was very new to all of this. I let Candice pay all the bills. Most of the times I wouldn't even look at the checks, but just sign them. In fact, the office checkbook was always with her. She would order supplies for the office, pay the rent and write checks for all the expenses for the maintenance of the office.

She decided that we should order soft drinks for the office staff. I thought it was customary, so I agreed to it. Later, I found out it was an expensive venture. Candice would order drinks every week rather than once a month as the agreement was. She would write a check and sometimes stamp my name on it. I knew it was not right, but I didn't want to annoy her, so I let it continue for a long time. This was least bit of my problem. Candice soon found out that the memory of typewriter was full. She printed about 40 to 50 papers to clear the memory of the typewriter. Most of them were love poems written by Linda. Apparently, she wrote them when she was with her boyfriend and a whole lot more when she broke up with him. In some of the poems she even mentioned him by name. It was very sad to learn about this situation. This also explained as to what she was doing behind my back. I did not read the poems, but Candice did. She informed me that Linda indeed had good writing skills. We decided to mail those poems to Linda. We didn't hear from Linda, but the poems were not returned to us either. So, we assumed that she got them.

Candice and Bonita made a good working team They got along very well. While going through the drawers we found stacks of superbills that had not been billed. It was shocking to know that the last time billing was done was before I left on maternity leave. I had become used to practicing without any revenues.

All my friends had told me to hang in there. Luckily Candice and Bonita were very good in billing. One weekend even I went to the office and helped them to catch up. We were billing by hand. In one weekend we were able to knock out a lot of billing. It was clear that none of the patients had gotten any statements from our office about the money they'd owed. This was the time when I learned how to bill different insurances. The office staff eventually caught up with it. Soon we started to get paid. I did not have to worry any more about this part of my practice.

I became healthy after childbirth and never had any significant medical problems. My daughter would sometimes tell her baby brother that Mom was allergic to you that's why she got so sick while he was in my tummy.

One day I saw a patient in the office for some neurological problems and when I saw his demographics, he had written homeless and had no telephone number or address. It touched my heart and I started to become very empathetic to his situation. I helped him medically as well as financially as much as I could. Soon he started to feel better. A few weeks later he showed up for his appointment to my office with four small kids and a wife. They all were dressed in heavy jackets and appeared as if they had not had a shower forever. I put the whole family in a room and sat down to discuss with them as to what was going on. He informed me that he was homeless and had no money whatsoever. He was afraid that if he did not seek help or find a place to live, his kids would be taken away from him. There was a real chaos in the office because I myself did not know who to approach and how to help this family. He did not just need money, but he also needed shelter, food, clothing and medical care for all of them. I called the social worker at the hospital and found some numbers. I made phone calls personally and instructed one of my employees to help the family. The social worker was able to refer them to local charities. He was later assigned a social worker who was able to handle most of their needs. This patient had come from out of town and had no relatives in Tulsa. I had no knowledge of his background at all. He was secretive about his past. He did not tell me where he came from, what he was doing prior to this or how he got in this situation. I still think that there was something mysterious in his life that he did not want to share. He never got back to me after that day. We tried to call the same social worker to find out if he made connection with them and got any help. Apparently, he never made it to the shelter and just disappeared from Tulsa. This haunted me for a long time, but I don't know if I could have done anything different.

Soon I became very busy both in the hospital and office. I was relatively young and had a zeal to succeed despite having two small kids. I would start early and go to the hospital at 7am-8am and then come have a busy day at the office.

§ * – FEEDING DESIRE

About a year later one day when I was rounding at Kaiser rehab, I got a call from my office on the hospital line. We did not have cell phones at that time. The office staff always knew my hospital schedule. Bonita was calling to inform me that she was leaving me as she had taken up another job. I came to the office to talk to her, but she had already made up her mind to leave. She did not even give a notice for two weeks which was mandatory. I couldn't do anything about it. She had already received her last paycheck the day before. I was worried but Candice was not. She hired one of her nieces to work for us temporarily. The two of them handled all the office affairs very well. Candice was very motherly to everybody. She would go to the cafeteria, bring food for me without even asking me and leave it on my desk so I could have lunch properly almost every day. Unfortunately, Candice and her niece had morbid obesity. Their eating habits were very unhealthy. Having a burger, fries and the largest cup of soda every day for lunch was a routine. Initially I was hesitant to tell Candice anything but later I informed her that I was a vegetarian, so she won't bring me food. By this time Hillcrest hospital started providing meals for physicians in a lounge adjacent to the cafeteria. This was a blessing. Firstly, the food was healthy and balanced and secondly it gave me a chance to sit and eat with other physicians. The meals were also free. Hillcrest hospital is the only place where doctors have had this privilege forever and ever.

I had started taking calls for the emergency room as well as for the hospital every third week. The schedule was very hectic and demanding. Around the same time, I was also admitting my own patients to Hillcrest Hospital which means I had to do the history and physical, daily rounds and even discharge them. The patients had to be discharged before noon if nothing was pending. One day one of my hospital patients was supposed to be discharged at noon, but one of the lab results was not available. Patient and I both waited all day and finally around 5:00 o'clock his result came back. So, it was ok for him to go home. Unfortunately, patient did not have any family members who lived in town. He was living in a facility for people with disability. He did not have a vehicle or the money to take a cab home. Usually in these kinds of situations the hospital will pay for the cab ride. Unfortunately, it was too late, and arrangements could not be made. It was late in the evening, and I was still in the hospital seeing consults when he spotted me. He explained the whole situation and asked if I could help him. I could have paid for a cab ride and sent him home. But I don't know why I didn't do that. I thought this patient would walk into an empty apartment all by himself after having been sick for several days. So, it was not proper for him to go by himself. I went to the cafeteria and got some food for him and offered to take him home in my own car. I left him at his apartment. His apartment was not in a very desirable part of Tulsa, and for a moment, I was a little bit apprehensive about going there late in the evening. Fortunately, everything worked out and my patient was very thankful to me for this. I thought about it afterwards and admitted to myself that it was a mistake. Either I should have asked somebody else to accompany me or I should have paid for his cab ride home. I contacted. his sister, who lived in Florida and explained the situation to her. She understood the gravity of situation because this could happen again. Patient was known to have seizures and had been admitted several times because of that. Finally, after a few months, the sister came to town and visited me in my office. It was our mutual decision that patient should not live alone. His sister took him with her to Florida to take care of him in future.

I had by this time made acquaintance with many of the doctors. They started referring patients to me in my office as well as consult me in the hospital for their patients with neurological problems. This is what a private practitioner wants to become busy and successful. There were a few general physicians who only did outpatient clinics and did not admit patients to the hospital. One of them was Doctor English. He would call me and ask me to admit his patients with acute neuro. problems to the hospital which I gladly did. I also saw several of his patients in the office. He was a very caring physician and always wanted to know what was happening to his patients. We spoke to each other several times a week. This was on top of me sending my evaluation report to him regularly.

We started to exchange Christmas gifts every year with many physicians. Over the years it became a big deal. We would order fruit baskets from a local store and then my staff was assigned to distribute those gifts to different doctor's offices if they were within driving distance. This became routine every Christmas. I would send out about 40 to 50 gifts and receive even more every year. After a few years it became difficult to continue this tradition. So, I decided to cut down on the number of gifts we were sending and only send gifts to a few of the physicians and friends.

During one of the Christmases, the girl who was assigned to deliver gifts and was given time off from the office, became ill. She had done it for several years and was very aware of the addresses and the general routine. The new person was a temporary hire. She was able to do the job most of the time, but occasionally she would need help. On one such day she asked for help as she couldn't figure out how to drive to Dr. English's office. I offered to drive her over there to his office. When we reached there, she got out of the car and took the gift to his office, and I stayed in the car in the driver's seat. That was perhaps the only doctor where I had to drive her to. After that, she was able to take care of it on her own. While we were driving back, I felt that I should have gone in to say hello to Doctor English. I was talking to him several times a week but had never met him. Ironically, I had never even seen a picture of him. His office was in north Tulsa a little far from the hospital and my office. He never came for any hospital meetings or functions. I felt awkward delivering Christmas gifts, so I was kind of hiding. That is why perhaps I didn't go in. Next year around March I got the news that Dr. English passed away after a brief illness. I did not know any details as to what happened to him later, I was told that he had a massive heart attack. I felt very bad because I never got a chance to see this man who supported me through my practice and spoke to me as if we were good friends several times a week.

With a sad heart I called his office and found out when the funeral would be. I went for the funeral and had a very depressive feeling that

I will be seeing his face for the first time when he's already deceased. I went to the church and as luck would have it was a closed cascade funeral. There was a big picture of him by the cascade and that's when I saw what Dr. English looked like.

His staff was very courteous to me and each one of them greeted me on this somber occasion.

It was a very sad experience for me. It brought me to realization that human beings don't last forever. Making contacts not just on phone but in person is very important. I still miss him.

One day out of the blue Candice got a call from Bonita. She wanted to know if she could be rehired as her new job was not going well. Candice was very fond of her and had kept in touch with her while she was working at another office. I had a feeling that Candice possibly encouraged her to reapply for the job at our office as her coworker who was her niece became pregnant and decided not to work. It was a blessing to have her back. After coming back, she appeared to be more mature and a better typist. This turned out to be a long-lasting relationship between all of us. We became like a family. I would order food sometimes and we would have a meal together. We would exchange gifts on Christmas, and we also celebrated birthdays. It was during one of these gatherings when we came to know that Bonita was only sixteen when she came to work for us initially.

Life was good for 2 years. I became comfortable and continued to work hard. Candice was very helpful and had a very nice personality. She was nice to my family too. She had one son who was very smart and later became a police officer.

I started going to India for three to four weeks during Summers as the kids were getting older. In my absence Candice and Bonita would take care of the office. I trusted Candice with everything, even the checkbook. She would pay all the bills, order supplies and write pay checks. I would sign the checks when they were ready. She would even calculate taxes and deductions. I noticed that sometimes in my absence she would write the paychecks and scribble my name. Because I had good relationship with the bank, the checks would go through without any problem. She had possession of the checkbook even when I was out of town. We had an accountant who filled taxes for the office. I never thought about it or became suspicious about any wrongdoing. I trusted her fully. Candice was like a mother hen who took care of everybody. She was very popular with the patients and knew lot of people in town. Her son who was a teenager at the time. She would often get phone calls from school but knew how to handle them without any problem or taking time off from work. Overall, her son was a good kid and never got in trouble. Unfortunately, because of morbid obesity she would sometimes slow down. She had already had gastric bypass surgery, but it didn't help. I regret that after having spent time with her for so long I never counseled her or even brought out the topic of obesity to her. Her dietary habits were very poor, and she also suffered from lack of activity. She was otherwise very smart and very good in her work and till today I think that she was the one who directed me to a right path so that I could continue my practice in a proper way. She often referred several of her family members to me for neurological care. So, over the next few years, I got to know many of her relatives and close friends. Some of them continued with me even after Candice's departure. I was always well informed about Candice's whereabouts.

On one Friday late in the afternoon while I was finishing my work at St John's Hospital, when I got a call from HR department. They wanted to see me immediately. I was asked to come to the director's office. When I went there, I was shown couple of prescriptions allegedly signed by me for a St. John's employee named Linda. It was signed as if it was written by me. On another prescription it was written and again signed by me that Linda who was supposedly my patient was sick and that she could not go to work for 10 days. I did not have any patient by that last name, nor did I write those prescriptions. Apparently, this had been going on for some time and that is how the HR at Saint John's hospital became suspicious. Linda was Candice's cousin. She had listed me as her PCP. She was getting pain medications allegedly prescribed by me on regular basis. She had been taking a couple of days off every so often, allegedly recommended by me. She would submit prescriptions written by me to her supervisor. I told them that those were not my signature, and I did not know anybody by that name. HR department had been suspicious for several months. This was the first time she was off was for 10 days. I was all set to go on vacation the next day which was a Saturday so nothing could be done.

I left for my vacation for a week as was planned not feeling very elated. The hospital HR chief was ok to wait for a week. When I came back to my office on following Monday, I called the police as was recommended by the HR personnel at St John's hospital. and explained everything to them. Candice was called to my office and was questioned for several hrs. by the police. She admitted to writing the note, but not the prescription for pain medication. I did not want to file charges as police wanted me to do. I decided to discuss this with Candice and told her everything. She thought it was best if she resigned and take care of the legal battle on her own. She was not arrested but was given a future appointment to appear in the court for further legal action. I was very disappointed and heartbroken because not only I trusted Candice, but she was also my friend. We did not have an argument, nor did I question her about anything. Next day she resigned, and I never saw her again for many years. I do not know what happened. I was asked repeatedly to press charges against her, but I refused.

After leaving my job, she did not work for several years and then she started working for a gastroenterologist. Apparently, she did a good job because she was with them for many years. She would often send me messages through her relatives who were still my patients.

I was very sad for next few days after this incidence, but I soon realized that I had to move on without her and with the help of new hire.

By now I had two kids one a newborn and another one five years old. There were occasions when the nanny would not show up and I had obligations at work. So, my husband and I decided that he would take half day off if nanny didn't show up instead of me not working at all, so the kids were taken care of. I had two ladies working for me for my kids.

My 5-year-old was becoming very inquisitive about my job and always wanted to go with me to the hospital during her school breaks. One day I had to do an EMG at doctor's hospital and decided to take her with me. I had to get permission from the CEO to bring my child to the hospital which he gladly allowed. I went to the EMG lab where the patient was on the table ready to have the test done. I had my daughter sit in a corner and instructed her not to talk while I started the procedure, she watched everything with astonishment and did not utter a word. After the procedure was done, she told me mommy I want to be like you. It came true because eventually when she grew up, she became a neurologist and did fellowship in movement disorder. She and I both remember her frequent encounters with patients in my office and in the hospital. That is how perhaps she got interested in neurology. She worked at my office off and on through high school and during summer vacation. She would often travel with me to outreach clinics and help me just like any of the other office personnel. While driving car I would often speak to her about different subjects. She always felt very special because in the clinic she was treated differently, and everybody respected her even though she was very young. I knew she was getting special treatment because she was my daughter. During one of our conversations, I told her that she should earn the respect and get special treatment because of her own merit and work and not because she is somebody's daughter. She often repeats this to me and still remembers that quote.

In the office we had a part-time help who later became a full-time employee. Bonita took over Candice's position and became very smart in handling everything. The practice was becoming very busy. I was working almost 12 hrs. a day. I even started going to Cushing on Wednesdays. I would take my EMG machine each time which was not easy to transport. I needed help. So, I started taking one of the secretaries with me. While I was out on Wednesdays the office staff would catch up with their work. I enjoyed my day out on Wednesdays, but after a few yrs. I realized that it was not a good business decision. Bonita became the advocate for the office staff which made them work together very well. I always listened to her and made changes as needed. We had to go to Oklahoma City to meet with Medicare officers and get special permission to do certain procedures in the office. It allowed me to do the test and follow up visit on same day.

At the suggestion of a colleague, we invested in a diagnostic center along with about fifteen other physicians. My job was to do EMG/NCV on all patients. It kept me very busy in the mornings. After having done it for about six months it was apparent that it was time consuming and was taking too much of my time away from my office. Most of these patients were referred by attorneys. I did not want to be associated with the legal issues, so I decided not to do these procedures. The whole investment turned out to be a losing proposition. I had to pay part of the loan for this venture so I could get out of this business deal

I always felt that I made a very nice, wise decision to have the office right by the hospital. It was easy for my patients to go to the emergency room if needed and go downstairs to get the blood test one. Sometimes patient would have the test done in the hospital and would come back to the office if they had any questions. One of my patients had a speech problem, secondary to a stroke. He was not weak in any part of his body. He, however, could communicate only with gestures. He could comprehend very well. Due to his inability to express himself; he was considered disabled. Most of the times he would be brought to the office by his son, his only child. After a few months, his son moved out of town and my patient was left at the mercy of the neighbors to bring him for his appointments and take him to hospital visits if a test was needed. He started having excessive drooling of saliva and swallowing difficulty. I scheduled him for a swallowing test at Hillcrest Hospital Radiology and explained everything to the neighbor who came with him. Apparently, on the day of the swallowing test, his neighbor dropped him at the hospital door and left with instructions for him to come down to the main gate after completion of the procedure. The patient came down in about an hour to be taken home after the procedure was done. However, he got turned around and could not go to the spot where he was supposed to meet the neighbor. He started to go up and down in different parts of the hospital. When he was finally spotted by the security he could not explain to security as to what was happening. The security guard searched his wallet and found my name and telephone number. They brought him to my office. We were able to get in touch with his neighbor. It was a happy ending. I'm thankful that the patient did not get lost and wander off to the street. Once again, I felt good that I was close by to be able to help. It was amazing for everybody to see that despite his speech problem, we had no problem communicating with him. He of course was very relived after seeing the familiar faces in my office.

It reminds me also of another situation where a patient by the name of Mr. Reed. developed a similar kind of stroke. He started to drive about 8-10 months after having stroke. But his speech never became legible. He felt so independent that he started to come to my office for his visits on his own. Initially his wife was very concerned and thought this was not going to work out because of lack of communication. He then started to write a little bit and felt even more confident about coming alone. Of course, his wife would call me after his visits, so I could explain to her as to what was happening. It was hilarious how much he and I could talk to each other He would not even finish a sentence and I could understand what he's saying. We were not just a patient and a doctor, but good friends including my staff. I always enjoyed visiting with him and to see him improve slowly but gradually.

§ * – IN THE SWING OF THINGS

The office was running very smoothly for next three years. Bonita's husband's office moved to Houston. Initially I was told that Bonita would stay in Tulsa with the kids and continue to work for me. That did not happen so within three months when the schools closed, she decided to move as well. She informed me ahead of time and stayed with me for almost a month. Even after her kids went to Houston with their father. She found two ladies and trained them very well. We both decided that it was best for the practice if Bonita continued to do the billing remotely. I had to be convinced as I had not done it before. We decided that I would send all the necessary paperwork to her couple of times a week and she would come to Tulsa every month to give me report. She would be available from 8:30am-5pm daily on phone if needed. This arrangement worked for us well. I opened an account with Federal express. I would personally send the package twice a week and always made sure that she got it in next two days. I was happy about the arrangement and almost bragged about it to my colleagues as to how efficiently billing and collection was being done. I never interfered too much with money matters nor did I ask too many questions about the reimbursements. Bonita came regularly every month initially. Later her visits became once every two to three months. I did not force her to come more frequently as I thought everything was going smoothly. My blind trust got me in trouble later.

We had Anita and Jackie taking care of the office with remote and consistent help from Bonita. Anita was trained to do the front office, meaning making appointments, obtaining demographic information from the patients, accepting co-pays and checking patients in and out. The other girl Jackie was supposed to be the helper. Her job was rooming patients and taking their vitals along with filing. As time passed both started to do each other's work. This had to be done because every Monday Anita would come around noon. She informed me that her father was sick, and she had to take him to VA hospital every Monday morning for his appointment. She was the only child of her widowed sick father. She was efficient, sincere and hard worker, so I did not object to her routine. Anita seemed to have some medical problems of her own. She had episodes where she would start sweating profusely and become very nervous so much so that she would leave work and go out but a few minutes She told me that she had hypoglycemia and had to eat on time. I witnessed a few of these episodes and became suspicious. I knew she was not telling the truth. I decided to hire another girl for the office to help as we were getting busier than before. Her name was Sheila. She was mature and experienced.

Bonita was now coming 3-4 times a year. She would educate me about insurance policy changes, look over the performance of the staff and talk to me about new billing codes. After vising with me she would go and attend a course which means I would not see her till the next day.

She also brought to my attention about the problems the other girls were having. We sometimes decided together about giving a raise to the staff members during these visits. If they had any grievances, she would bring them to my attention. I would take her out to doctor's lounge for lunch or sometimes close the office for an hour and take everyone out. We were like a family, and I was enjoying the closeness they provided.

During one of her visits, she told me that she had noticed that money was missing from window collection. She confronted Jackie as she was responsible for handling money. She admitted to taking money from the office when she needed it. She also informed us that whatever money she took she would eventually bring it back and put it in the collection. This was not acceptable to me, so I took her away from the front office and asked her to do only filing and room the patients. Her weekly hours were reduced from 40 to 30. After a few weeks I got a call from Jackie's husband threating me that if I did not give her 40 hours per week, he would take me to court. At that time, I decided to let her go which did not sit well with her husband who was a big, tall muscular guy. He was himself employed and was making good salary as I had been previously informed. Jackie immediately filed for unemployment. She even got it because she had small children. I did not contest it for the same reason.

Eventually I found out that Anita was heavily into drugs. Sometimes she even had withdrawal seizures while at work. We had to let her go when she admitted to this problem. It seems she was on probation for few years and had to go to her probation officer every Monday. She went back to abusing drugs as soon as her probation was over. One day I saw her in that state and asked her to go to emergency room. She refused and stayed in a room in the office. Later one of the other girls took her home. Next day she did not show up for work. So, I asked

Bonita to call her and tell her that we did not need her services anymore.

§ * – MARYANN

Luckily, I had already hired Maryann as I had a hunch that Anita was not capable of handling her duties. I was actually very lucky. I advertised in Tulsa world and only one person applied. I hired her and she turned out to be an excellent employee.

Sheila and Maryann got along very well. Both were married but did not have any children They were very devoted to their jobs. Sheila brought her own radio and some coffee mugs and seemed very settled in the office. Maryann did not talk much but worked diligently. Bonita liked them and decided to train them as usual. This continued for almost a year. We decided that once a month I would take all of them out for lunch. We enjoyed our free time together. We laughed, told jokes and even dressed up on that day. The girls were always picking a new restaurant every time. I paid for these lunches each time. Later I realized that altogether it was not a good business decision. I was always against closing office for lunch or for any other reason during working hours. So, we decided to order food and eat in the office. We still had a good time. Sometimes we would all cook and bring a dish. A few months later Mary Ann decided to go on vacation for a week with her husband starting Saturday. On Monday Sheila did everything all by herself without any problem. Bonita was also helping remotely.

On Tuesday which was supposed to be our new patient day I walked into the office through the back door like I always did and noticed that the lights were off, and it was very quiet. When I went to the front office, I noticed that there was no one in the front office. I called her home several times but there was no answer. The patients started to arrive. I had no idea about their co-payments or any details about their insurance. The charts were pulled and each one of them had a blank charge sheet. I informed the patients that everybody will be seen but copayments will not be collected. The tests would be scheduled soon, and no one had to worry about me being alone. It was a very hectic day, and I was glad that it was over. Patients were very cooperative. It was the month of July. Schools were close. I called my Nanny and asked her to bring my ten years old daughter to my office. When she came, I trained her for a few minutes mainly about answering the telephone and put her to work. She was supposed to say Tulsa neurology and headache clinic, may I help you. After this she would take a message and write it down. She was not to ask any questions or solve any problems. After an hour or so she was also able to make return appointments. My daughter was thrilled and from then on came to my rescue several times.

Sheila's husband called around 5pm when he reached home and saw so many missed calls from my office. He had no idea where Sheila had gone. It seems she took some of her stuff and drove away. He informed me that they were having problems in their marriage and Sheila had indicated that she was going to leave him. I never heard anything from Sheila or her husband after that day. Her last paycheck was mailed to her residence. Stuff that she left in the office was never collected by her. I still have the coffee mugs she brought to the office. Her radio was used by the new staff for a long time.

Fortunately, Maryann came back from her mini vacation on Wednesday. We hired temporary help from a Staffing agency because it was apparent that one girl could not take care of everything. I had never worked with any agency before. I was told that I had to pay the agency directly for three months and if I liked the secretary, I could hire her for a permanent position. It sounded like a good idea, so I agreed. It did not work out as I thought it would. A week later May the temporary hire did not show up. She refused to pick up her phone when we tried to call her. I complained to the staffing agency. I was later told that May decided not to work at another doctor's office as we were too busy for her liking. To my surprise I was also informed that I would have to pay her salary to the staffing agency as per our contract which I did. Since then, I have never hired any one through these kinds of agencies. I always advertised in Tulsa world when I needed office position filled.

Within a week we also hired Paula who was elderly, single, very talkative and had a very exuberant personality. She came on time but was very slow. It took her a long time to understand the way our office operated even though she had told me that she was experienced. She had tremors of her hands at times. She wanted some gadgets to function. She also needed a soft cushion to sit on, thumb gloves to turn the pages, long pens to write, a footrest and a chair that would lean back. I let her order stuff that we did not have in the office as it was not a big deal. I bought her the chair that she asked for and gave her an office check signed by me and asked her to go to Office Depot and buy rest of the things she needed. She had only mentioned about small petty things that she required to write and be comfortable while at work. She went shopping at the end of the day and next morning brought a receipt for $125 that she had spent at Office Depot. I was not familiar with the gadgets she bought at my expense. I felt foolish for trusting a new person with a blank check. I decided never to do this again. We had colorful pencils with long attachments, couple of cushions with absurd writings on them, several quotes written on wooden handles, thumb gloves, hand lotion and several other things that I don't care to remember.

We had drug reps bringing us small gifts and food almost every day which is not done these days. It was always customary for the food to be shared. I always discouraged acceptance of gifts from anybody. The staff brought it to my attention that whenever anything was brought to the office by the drug reps It was always accepted by her. And soon it would disappear before anybody could see it. I noticed that she was hiding all these things under the table not realizing that when she sat it was pushed from the other side, and everybody could see it. It was hilarious, and the other girls had fun with it every day. At the end of the day, she would put all that stuff in her big bag and take it home. None of the girls ever objected to it as they were not interested in any of the stuff that was being brought.

By then at the advice of Maryann we also hired Stephanie who was going to school in the evening to become a nurse but wanted to work during daytime. She was very smart and did not take much time to train. As luck would have it, just when things were going well for two years Maryann had to leave to take care of her mother who was very sick and needed care 24/7. She decided not to work and take care of her mother full time.

Stephanie and Paula did not get along. They fought almost every day. it was obvious that most of the caseload was being managed by Stephanie and Paula was just doing a little bit of typing and filing. she brought her lunch from home and took forever to finish it. She also would involve herself in personal problems of the patients and carry-on long conversations which were not related to their office visits. In fact, that took time away from her office work. Stephanie on the other hand would come a little bit late in the morning as she had to attend a class and leave around 4:00 o'clock. Despite that, she was able to. finish all the work that was assigned to her and some that was supposed to be finished by Paula. Obviously, Stephanie got very sick of it and one day she let Paula have it behind my back. She told Paula that she was lazy and was not capable of working in an office setting. Paula got very mad and decided to leave the same day. Stephanie reassured me that she would take a few days off from school and make sure that everything was done properly till we hire a new person. At that time, I decided that we will have three persons working in the office no matter what. it was obvious that the office was getting busier by the day and two persons were not able to take care of the workload.

Gloria and Linda came aboard within a few weeks. The next six months went well. Stephanie worked very well with both. She was flexible and despite studying for her exams she kept on coming to work as much as she could. This was a great help for training the new employees. There was no chaos in the office.

Gloria however turned out to be a slow learner. She needed lot of training. She apparently had worked at a doctor's office as a filing clerk but put it on her resume as having experienced in handling front office.

I was never able to get her references. Linda and I decided that we will train her according to what we need and what we wanted her to do in the office, to which I agreed. Stephanie really surprised me with her leadership skills. She literally took over the office. After she finished her exams, and while she was waiting for her results, she worked full time and for once we had three full time employees. She finished nursing school and soon was offered a job at a hospital. It was a part time job, so she continued working at our clinic for next six months.

Linda was a good worker and things went smoothly for several months. I trusted her fully. One day I came back to the office unexpected and saw her leaving with copy paper under her arms. She informed me that she would pay me for it next day. I didn't mention anything about it ever and ignored it as it was not a big deal. She however lost my trust from then on. It was good because I learned my lesson and from then on, I started ordering the supplies for the office all by myself. So, I had complete control over the inventory. Gloria came to the office with a big trolley every day, she had so much stuff in her trolley as if she was ready to travel. I never knew what she brought in it or what she took home.

Linda fell off a step stool while she was trying to pull some files from a shelf. She hurt her ankle. She immediately went to Hillcrest Hospital emergency room for treatment. She soon found out that Hillcrest Hospital emergency room was not a covered facility by the Workman's Comp insurance. She got very upset when they started sending her the bills. I had already asked her to find out the names of clinics which accepted Workman's Comp insurance. She ignored it and continued to go to Hillcrest emergency room. Nobody had ever filed a workman's comp in my clinic. So, I had no idea how to handle it. She however soon sorted it out and her medical bills started getting paid. By now she was missing lot of work as she had to go to the chiropractor's office quite often.

Gloria was a subordinate of Linda and did not have any capability of initiating a task or even a conversation. Linda had started taking advantage of Gloria's weakness. So much so that Gloria would often lie for her, which I realized very late in the game. When I would call in the morning and ask for Linda, I was told that she had gone to the hospital to get coffee. I have always had a habit of contacting the office employees at 8:30 in the morning. Every morning at 8:30. Gloria was the only one calling me. She would check in for herself and Linda every day. To my utter surprise, I found out that Linda was coming late daily, and Gloria was covering up for her for reasons only known to her. At that time, I made a rule that every morning at 8:30a, the office staff would call me and inform me who all were there and about the schedule for the day, and if I had any new consultations in the hospital.

One day around 3:30pm, I left my office to go for rounds at the hospital. Soon I realized that I had forgotten one of my bags. I came back and called Gloria from my car to see if she could bring my bag downstairs. She told me that Linda was in the bathroom, and she won't be able to do it for the next few minutes. I agreed and didn't say anything. After a few minutes I called the office again and this time I asked for Linda because I knew she would come down with my bag immediately. I was again told that Linda was in the bathroom. I did not want to go upstairs and decided to wait for the bag to be brought to me. I knew something was not right, but I could not figure it out. By the time I called the last time, it had been 20 minutes. Gloria kept telling me that Linda had an upset stomach, so she was still in the bathroom. I decided to drive away to the hospital as it was getting late. In my heart of hearts, I knew something was not right and Gloria was lying to me, but I was not prepared to face the drama. I barely drove for a minute from the office when I saw Linda walking to her car with several bags full of groceries in Reasor's parking lot which is not very far from the hospital. Apparently, Linda had left the office a long time ago for grocery shopping while Gloria was lying for her, and I was waiting downstairs in the car.

I did not mention anything about this to Linda or Gloria. I knew that they were both covering for each other, and Linda was making use of Gloria's lack of intelligence and integrity. I started calling the office regularly in the mornings, sometimes I would also look at the timesheet. That is the time I found out that the person who comes to the office first clocked in for the second person and sign in a scratchy way so no one could recognize the signatures. I was getting disgusted with this kind of behavior because I never knew people would cheat just to get paid for 15 to 20 minutes

Gloria one day became belligerent when she was questioned about not finishing her task. She accused me that I did not have workman's comp and I was lying about it and that is why Linda had problem in getting her hospital bills being paid. Gloria was screaming on top of her voice trying to intimidate me. I almost thought of calling security, but it was almost 5:00 o'clock and after screaming her guts off, she left. To my utter surprise. Linda did not react to it and stayed calm pretending to finish her work at that time. I decided that I had to get rid of both employees but one at a time as I could not take care of the office business by myself. I even spoke to Bonita about it, who was gracious enough to offer to come and help me. So, the next day I went to the office at around 8:15 and waited for Linda and Gloria to come. Linda came in first. I did not tell her anything but just sat in the front office with her asking about the schedule, etc.

When Gloria arrived with her big trolley full of stuff, I did not let her come into the office and through the window told her that she could leave and that her employment had ended. She called her husband screaming and yelling to inform him that she had been fired. She used some very. derogatory names for me while she was talking to him. She finally left. Before leaving she informed me that she was going to go to unemployment office straight. She filed for unemployment. As a matter of fact, Linda wrote a letter to the unemployment office explaining to them about the behavior that Gloria had exhibited on her last day of employment. Gloria had been reprimanded three times previously and on each of those papers her signatures were present. This also helped in her not getting the unemployment. I did not care whether she got it or not.

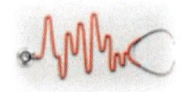

§ * – DOING BETTER BY HEART

One day I got a phone call from police checking about a patient. Apparently, this person went to a convenience store and passed out. He didn't have a wallet or a telephone. They found my name written on his health ID bracelet. He was known to have seizures. Luckily, I was able to guide EMSA personnel who stabilized him before taking him to ER. They were capable of doing this without my help, but I was able to provide them information about his family which helped.

A few years after I started going to a newly opened Cancer treatment center of America. I was invited to be a neurologist for in patients consults. I always enjoyed going to this hospital for several reasons. The first one was that it was a very beautiful facility at a very convenient location. It had good reputation and most of all I liked the patient population that it catered to.

There was always live music playing close to the entrance. Coffee and snacks for patients and relatives were provided. Comfortable seating and plenty of help was easily available to those who needed it. The families of patients could eat almost free at the cafeteria while rooming at highly discounted hotels. The hospital was very well planned. The patients came from different parts of America. They were given free transportation to come to the hospital and even to come for follow up visits after discharge. I knew almost all the doctors there and found them very friendly and very competent. I developed a special feeling for the patients who were all very sick. They needed Electrophysiological testing done which was not available in the hospital yet. So, they would be transported to and from my office by their escort service. My office staff was extra courteous and careful in handling these patients, who were very sick and very dependent. for most of the activities of daily living. Sometimes my office staff would wait for the patients downstairs while they were getting in and out of the limousine that transported them. We also made special arrangements for their I/V Poles to be hung and made sure that they were not in any discomfort while the procedure was being done. I made a lot of friends while I was doing the procedures and while I was practicing at cancer treatment center.

One of the patients would often ask me about Indian food availability in Tulsa. She told me that she was very fond of Indian cuisines especially since she got sick. It was very unusual as most of cancer patients lose their appetite. She was wanting to have the flavored food even more than before. We only had one Indian restaurant in Tulsa at that time So, I approached the owner of the restaurant, who was very well known to me, to see if he could deliver food at the hospital. He informed me that he will get the food ready but would not be able to deliver. I went and got the food and brought it to the patient. She was thrilled beyond mention to have the food and to be able to consume it with the permission of her oncologist and the therapists. Even though I ordered only a few dishes, the restaurant owner made sure that he sent a portion of most of the things that were available in the restroom. When I saw the food after it was opened, I could not believe the amount of food that was packed. More than half of it, I never ordered or paid for. The patient and her family appreciated it very much.

Another incident happened at the same hospital, which I still remember like it happened yesterday. One of the patients was almost terminal. She come to Tulsa from West Coast. She. expressed a desire to her family that she wanted to have a traditional Thanksgiving. Unfortunately, most of us, including her family, knew that most likely she would not make it to thanksgiving next year. Many of her family members and even close friends, for this reason, decided to fly to Tulsa for Thanksgiving and rent a room in a hotel so she could have a traditional Thanksgiving surrounded by her loved once. She did not want to go to a hotel and insisted on having the celebration at home. She wanted to be with her family and friends possibly for her last Thanksgiving. None of her relatives lived locally. Most people in the hospital were aware of her desire. So, when it was brought to my knowledge, I decided to act upon it. I went and approached the patient and the family members who were around her and offered my house for the get together. My own family was also in town, and we had already planned Thanksgiving like every year. It was mutually decided that the family of the patient would take the front of the house along with kitchen, spend about four hours and then leave.

I decided to have Thanksgiving dinner for my family after they left. I knew if I planned well and prepped the night before I could do it. They catered the food and brought everything with them. to my house. We shut the doors separating the front and the back of the house and let them have a personal time. About 50 people came for the celebration. The patient arrived happy, looking pretty wearing a beautiful head scarf. During those four hours, I never went to see as to what was happening. I had given my telephone number to patient's children so they could call me if they needed anything. I told them that I was available. They never asked me for anything. From the food to the drinks to the silver ware everything they had brought. After 4 hours when they left the house was spic and span and nobody could tell that there were 50 people in these rooms just a few hours ago. The note that they left for me was so overwhelming and full of emotions that I could not help but cry when I read it. If I'm ever asked in my life my best experience as a doctor, I would mention this one. Linda helped the family in planning the event including the catering service.

Bonita came from Houston for couple of days and helped Linda. With office work. She was very efficient in finding help for the office. Within next one week we hired Deborah and Lily.

Linda's husband had already been living in Lawton. She was very graceful to stay for at least six weeks and train Deborah and Lily

Deborah was the manager and apparently had lot of experience working in doctors' offices. Lily was checking patients in and out and helping Deborah when needed. She was told specifically that her working hours would be from 8:30am to 5pm. On payday, hours for each employees including the EEG technicians were submitted to me for my signatures and then they were faxed to the accountant. Next day he would bring the paychecks to us. Things were going smoothly.

I had a habit of sitting in the office after 5 o'clock to finish my dictation and read EEG. I'd never leave the office before 6 or 6:30pm. One day I saw Debra sitting on a bench outside the building when it was very cold at about 6pm. At that time Deborah informed me that she and her live-in boyfriend had only one vehicle. He brought her at 7am every morning to work and picked her up at 7pm. She had to sit outside till it was time to open the office doors. I felt, very bad for Deborah because the weather was turning very cold, especially in the morning and evening. I allowed her to come to the office at 7am. and stay there till 7pm. So, she would not have to sit in the cold weather outside the building. She was told specifically that our working hours were from 8:30am to 5pm with 30 minutes of lunch. She was not expected to do anything before 8:30am or after 5pm. She was very appreciative of this arrangement and thanked me multiple times because now she was sitting in a comfortable office and not fighting the cold weather every morning and evening.

During those hours when she was alone, she started to keep a log of hours which would start at 7am and end at 7pm. One day she informed me that she was not being paid for 12 hours a day that she was putting in everyday from 7am to 7pm. Bonita had a talk with her which did not work. Then I tried to clarify the situation that the only reason that she was allowed to come to the office early and stay late was because I was trying to help her because she didn't have her own vehicle. That did not work either. She decided to sue me and filed a case against me in the court.

I had to hire an attorney who tried to negotiate so, we would not have to go to the Court, but Deborah was adamant that she was owed money for the work that she had put in the office

We had no solution to this problem. At the suggestion of my attorney, we decided to pursue it. I went to Tulsa courthouse with my attorney on the appointed date. I was absolutely astonished to see Deborah, who looked very presentable in the office, but in the court, she was looking like a very different person. She was dressed in a sleeve less very loose-fitting long dress. She was not wearing a wig. She had multiple sores on her scalp. She did not have her usual makeup or jewelry on. She was wearing bathroom slippers and was carrying a grocery bag full of official documents. She almost appeared like she was homeless.

She presented the time sheets to the judge claiming that her work started at 7a and ended at 7p. She had very methodically made copies of the logbook that we had in the office. Unfortunately for her, none of these log sheets were authenticated by my signatures as was always done before the accountant would issue checks for all the employees. Fortunately for me the case was thrown out of court.

One day when I was working in the office late in the evening, as I often did, when around 6pm I got a call on my private line. That number was known only to the employees and me. I picked up because I thought that one of the girls probably wanted to say something to me. It was Deborah calling me from downstairs. She said, "I know you are there and when you come down, I will take care of you." I was very scared and thought she was going to harm me. I called Jessie the head of security at Hillcrest Hospital who escorted me to my car. Deborah must have spotted us because she never came close to me. From then on, she did not call me or threaten me. Jessie took it upon himself to provide me and my staff extra security measures in my office. He also arranged for security cameras to be placed where I parked. I am and will always remain indebted to him for making my workplace so secure for me and my staff.

I made it a point from then on not to stay back after 5 p.m. I started to always leave the office along with the other staff. Occasionally I would ask for an escort if I had to walk to my car late in the evening while I was working late in ER or hospital.

We hired Billy, Samantha. and Dylan. All of them had small children but no husbands. That turned out to be a positive thing. They would all sometimes meet in the evenings and or during weekends and have play dates for their kids. Dylan was part time and the other two were working full time. Lucky for me, every time I lost an employee, the other one came right behind her. Billy was very sweet. She would bring me small but very thoughtful gifts and leave them on my desk. The best was a Valentine's Day card with couple of pieces of candy on it. I really loved it. The gift did not mean much, but the gesture was very heartwarming to me. I reciprocated as much as I could. We made it a point to have couple of hours off once a month on Fridays. We would all eat together or sometimes even go out to eat and mingle.

On one of those Fridays, when we were supposed to go out for lunch, I got a call from a colleague who wanted me to see one of her patients the same day because he was having severe headaches. We cancelled the lunch and decided to bring the patient to the office immediately. He was a young man who had never had headaches like this before. In the past two days he was doubling up with pain despite taking several over-the-counter medications. His neurological exam was normal. But his pain was very acute. So, I decided to admit him in the hospital so that he could have all the tests done fast and get IV medications. His medical insurance wanted him to be only admitted to St. John's hospital. I called them and scheduled a stat MRI of the brain. I saw him in the office at three o'clock and at five o'clock his MRI was completed. The radiologist called me to inform me that this patient had Glioblastoma Multiforme. It came as a shock to me. The prognosis is always grave in this situation. It was with the help of my front office staff that we were able to make a diagnosis this quickly and get proper and timely help for this patient.

Doctor Larry Reed who had always been my supporter, hired several physicians from out of town to provide primary and specialty care in hospital and on outpatient bases. I became friends with most of his new hires. One of them was Doctor Gary Davis. He was admitting patients to Hillcrest and would often call me for consults. I was also getting referrals from him in my office. I met Dr. Davis initially in one of the meetings and then several times in the hospital parties and many official gatherings.

Unfortunately, he started having problem with his neck and consulted me for the same. I got detailed neurological work up on him but decided to treat him conservatively. He then had further testing done by a neurosurgeon who initially decided not to operate on him but because Dr. Davis was having severe neck pain, it was their mutual decision to go ahead with cervical discectomy. He had multiple neck surgeries and finally ended up having cervical fusion. He never recovered from this surgery and started to have pain and weakness in all the limbs so much so that within a few months he became quadriplegic, and wheelchair bound. He had lot of complications and finally his body gave up and he passed away.

This was a loss of an excellent physician and a very good friend. It hurt me for quite some time. He went to Dartmouth medical school and there he completed residency in internal medicine. He was always interested in research apparently even during residency. He managed to obtain research grant for treatment of HIV which was very prevalent at the time. I personally never spoke to him; however, through media information I came to know about his pending invention. Of course, it was difficult to implement his treatment in the USA because he did not have FDA approval. He started to travel to different countries including Africa and offer his treatment. His treatment was approved in some smaller continents who had a large patient population inflicted with this deadly disease. After coming back from Africa, he became more vocal about his invention. He would often tell us how well the patients were doing. He started to involve a couple of other doctors in his project. Unfortunately, all of this came to a halt after his demise.

During the summertime I always went to India with my children for a month. During my absence the office was supposed to be open. All the office personals were assigned duties to catch up with their paperwork. After coming back one summer I was informed by some patients that while I was gone, the office was like a daycare center. There were small kids running around everywhere, food was in the waiting room and all over the front office, loud music would be playing. I was informed about all of this by occasional patients would randomly walk into our office to get labs or medical records. When I came back, I did not tell the office staff that I knew what was happening while I was gone because I had no confirmation and I felt that it was not nice to blame them for something that I had not witnessed. I had learnt my lesson but continued with summer travel to visit my elderly parents.

It is not unusual for the front office staff to move from job to job for reasons only known to them. They would go to another job if they got paid just a few cents more an hour. It happened to me several times especially after coming back from time off.

I managed to hire Julie and Darlene after losing two out of three girls at the same time. To this date I feel that Candice and Julie were two of my best employees.

Darlene had very unusual, but interesting stories to tell about her life. She was born in Germany. Her American father while posted in Germany met her mother. They never got married. She was raised by her mother but always knew about her father. Growing up she never saw her father who lived in California. She started to exchange letters with him after finishing high school and became very fond of him. He finally invited her to come to California and visit him. She flew from Germany enroute to California. Due to some major technical problems the airplane made an unscheduled landing in Tulsa. At the airport she was stranded for several hours. She met a gentleman who was of

Mexican heritage and was working at one of the airport restaurants. She was treated very well by this young man .She was so charmed by him that she decided not to go to California and instead stay in Tulsa with him .She eventually got married to him and joined her husband in a family restaurant business which did not flourish .She went to school and got trained as a front office assistant .She was proficient in typing and spoke English fluently .Fortunately for me Julie and Darlene became very good friends. I liked them a lot. I started hanging out with them to joke around for a few minutes before leaving almost every evening. Julie was relatively quiet and did not talk much about herself. She had experience and good credentials. She got hired the day she came for an interview.

I had always made it a rule that I would never invite my office staff to my house and would always keep my personal life and business life separate. After I hired Julie and Darlene, I broke my own rule. More, to which, my husband 's 50th birthday was approaching. I asked my staff for some suggestions to plan the event. They came up with excellent ideas and helped me through and through. His birthday party was at home. We hired a dancer to come and dance at his birthday party with the instructions that she would be decently dressed and not make any unacceptable moves to which she agreed. So, on the day of the surprise party, one of my husband's best friends came and took him to play tennis. In the meantime, all the vendors came and brought the food. Darlene and Julie also came to my house. At around. 6:00 o'clock when my husband entered the house all of guests were there to surprise him.

In the meantime. Darlene whom my husband had never met started getting close to my husband pretending as if she knew him. My husband was very uncomfortable with the situation. She told him that she was a caterer and had brought the food for the party. My husband was blushing and was trying to stay away from her as much as he could when suddenly the hired German dancer walked in. She had regular clothes on till the music became loud and she started to pretend to get out of her clothes which she didn't as per my instructions. She also made my husband very uncomfortable. That day, I realized that the Germans could really dance. Both the girls were very helpful and stayed back till the party was over and the house was all put together.

§ * - TRAVELING

My office has always been in a building close to the hospital. The building got sold to a private investor, but hospital retained ownership of seven offices in the building and one of the offices was mine. They were very generous and charged me only nominal rent for many years. I was always very thankful to them for this generosity. Not only that, but they also provided me free Internet. One day while when my office was full of patients and as always, I was busy, suddenly two men in black suits and one woman in a similar attire showed up. My secretary informed me that they wanted to see me. I was scared as to what happened that people were coming to my office at this time Those days agents from Oklahoma Bureau of narcotics and controlled drugs were conducting raids in different offices and founding stuff that was not very nice. I knew that I had nothing to worry about but still I was almost shaking by the time I sat down to start a conversation with them. I could not believe that those persons from the hospital staff had come just to tell me that from now on the hospital will not be paying for my Internet and I had to arrange for my own account. They also informed me that this was not just me, but they were doing this to several physicians who had been getting free internet from the hospital. I was relieved, elated and very happy to pay for the Internet and thankful to God that this was just a minor incidence and nothing detrimental to my practice.

One of the patients from Cushing introduced me to her nephew, who had been having seizures and lived in Albuquerque. He happened to be in Cushing at the time, so I got a chance to treat him. He became well and his seizures were controlled. This impressed her mother so much that she started bringing him to see me from Albuquerque. almost every year. At that time, I found out that his sister also had seizures for many years. So, from one it became two patients coming every year. Somehow it blossomed into at least 10 patients who were coming to me from. Albuquerque at different times for seizure control and many other neurological problems. I used to joke that instead of those people coming to see me. Perhaps I should fly to Albuquerque and take care of them. Once a few of them rented a van to come to Tulsa to see me. They were all very nice people and became very dear to me. I would often pay them money to have lunch and help them in many ways I could. Once while I was home sick with flu. I got a call from the office that two of the patients from Albuquerque had not gotten a message about me not being in the office and had arrived. We were in a dilemma. I was sick and could not go to the office for next few days. They would either stay in a hotel and pay so much money or go back without treatment. Julie took it upon herself and drove the patients and their charts to my home. I saw them in my home Office and did what needed to be done. Not only me but the patients also remained very appreciative of what Julie did.

I had to take my EMG machine with me which I could not handle by myself so, we decided that Julie would bring the EMG machine and meet me in Sapulpa. We would transfer it to my car and then both of us would drive to Cushing together to see patients. After the clinic we would go for lunch every Wednesday. We started talking to each other about lot of things. During one of our trips to Cushing she told me that she was an abused child. Her father would be sitting in the living room opposite her mother in the same room when he would ask Julie to sit in his lap under the blanket. He would abuse her right in front of her mother. She always thought that her mother knew what was going on but did not have the guts to confront her father. Through her teenage years the intensity of abuse both sexual and physical continued for a long time. It haunted her that she was abused in the presence of her mother, but she didn't have the courage to talk to her because of her father's threats. As per Julie when she was about 14, she got a chance to go out of town as a cheerleader for her school. When she asked for permission from her father, he made a deal. She had to please him in the bathroom, only then she would be allowed to go on this trip. Julie did as she was asked to and went on this trip. She was very scared of her father and the threats he made. She never had the guts to tell any of her friends, family or her teachers about the abuse. This pattern continued for many years till Julie had enough of it. After graduating from high school, she ran away from home and soon became pregnant at a very young age. Her parents never came looking for her as she moved far away to another city. She thought that she had hit a jackpot because her boyfriend at that time was older, loving, caring and a good provider. He would shower her with gifts that she had never seen or imagined in her life. He bought her a big diamond ring and a nice car. Julie had always walked everywhere while she was at home.

When her daughter was about a year old suddenly one day the police came charging into their house and arrested her boyfriend. Apparently, he was a drug dealer making a lot of money. Perhaps that was the reason that he could shower Julie with expensive gifts. She was vulnerable and was attracted to him for wrong reasons. At least that's what she thought. Later, she realized that she was in love with this guy and continued to feel that way for many years to come. Her boyfriend was convicted of first-degree murder of a young man and was given life sentence with no possibility of parole.

She continued to visit him in prison and never stopped loving him. All these experiences made Julie very mature when she was only about 19 years old. She started to fear for her and her daughter's life when the other drug dealers started to haunt her. She had no choice but to move back close to her hometown. She was very sore about her past. She visited her father a few years later when he was dying and asked him to confess in front of her mother about the abuse. She wanted this clarification bad, but it never happened because her father never confessed and passed away. Her mother never believed her and instead blamed her for everything. In next few years she went through several more abusive relationships and finally started living with another African American gentleman who was gainfully employed as a janitor in a hospital. She had two children with him who were very bright. He proposed to her several times, but Julie had decided that she was never going to be in a committed relationship. She wore the engagement ring and was still looking for boyfriends. She would sometimes go on a date behind her current live in boyfriend's back. She would talk about these dates and the excellent time she had. Darlene always knew everything about these encounters. Julie often said that her live-in boyfriend would always be only a friend as in her opinion he was not a husband material. There was also a rumor that he was also having a relationship with another woman but would always come home to Julie. It was an intricate love affair, which was difficult to understand.

Darlene had one son who was not doing very well in school. Darlene and her husband were very fond of gambling. By then we had casinos in Tulsa.

I had the habit of going to the bank every Friday to withdraw money for the entire week. I started to notice that my money was missing. Initially I justified it by thinking that I spent it or did not withdraw the amount I thought I did. I would often come up with different reasons to justify that there was not any problem. In the long run, I realized my money was being stolen from my handbag which I would keep in a cabinet. The only persons who knew about this were Julie and Darlene. Since I never witnessed anyone taking money from my purse, I could not accuse any one of them. I knew Julie would not do this. She sold her plasma every few weeks to make extra cash.

Darlene was a die-hard fan of Pittsburgh Steelers. She made almost a shrine around her desk while the game was going on. She would hang Pittsburgh Steeler's shirt, shoes and a hat all around her desk and wear their logo shirt. I was not very particular about staff wearing scrubs during those days. They could wear anything they wanted to if it was professional. It was fun to see her so elated while the Pittsburgh Steelers were playing. If they won a game, then it was really a party in the office. She had also learned art of tarot cards. She would read cards for me and for Julie for fun. I don't think she knew anything about this game. We just played along for fun. She would come up with funny stories and predictions to make us laugh. It was nice and healthy to work with them. About once a month whenever we could I would take them out for lunch for gourmet meals.

After our Cushing clinic. Julie and I always went for lunch and again visited with each other. I always felt that Julie had a special place in my heart. It was surprising to me that despite having undergone so much stress in her life and having had a difficult childhood, she was still. very pleasant, smart, sincere worker and honest

Darlene started having problem with her son. He ran away from home and could not be found for several months. Later when he was found he was heavily into drugs. He had lot of legal problems and was taken to a juvenile detention center. He stayed there for a long time. Darlene decided to quit her job and stay at home to take care of him. Julie was alone in the office so within a few days we hired Casey.

Casey was short, charming and a heavyset female who was ready to please everybody. Our office opened daily at 8:30 and closed at 5pm. She had taken permission from me to come at 8 and leave at 4:30 instead of 5pm. One day in the morning Julie had not arrived yet and I was making round in the hospital when Casey came to the office and passed out. When Julie arrived, she found her laying on the floor convulsing. She was taken to ER for treatment. None of us knew that Casey had brittle diabetes. She had an episode of hypoglycemia which resulted in a seizure. From then on, I decided to get a medical history from the applicants. Casey started having the spells very frequently and decided to leave. We hired Angela. She also had medical problems about which she did not mention on her application. I noticed that she was drinking fluids almost all the time. She even made me buy big bottles of water for her, so she did not have to bring water bottles from home every day. She was a good worker but appeared to be very authoritative and demanding.

Julie got along very well with her. Angela and Julie would often get together in the evenings and some weekends. Angela worked for us for almost a year. One day she didn't show up. It was not like her to take off without calling the office. Julie later that day found out that her husband suddenly left her that morning with all his stuff. Julie and I drove to her house to console her and take some food for her. She was devastated, depressed, emotional and upset. She came back to work but couldn't continue. She apparently needed a kidney transplant, and her husband did not want to support her. He filed for divorce and Angela left her employment. Angela wanted her ex-husband to pay hefty alimony as per Julie's information.

My business was growing but the frequent change of staff was affecting it. Bonita came from Houston and helped Julie. She also helped me hire two new employees Vivian and a gentlemen named Ketan. Vivian was experienced having worked in a clinic before. She could type and was very mannered and pleasant with the patients. Ketan was an east Indian young man from California. He had met a Caucasian girl from Owasso and decided to move to Oklahoma. He had very impressive credentials. He however was very lazy. He started missing work and either come late or left early. He lasted only two months. Julie was running the office with great zeal. Vivian was also doing very well.

Two months later when I came back from a week's vacation, I came to know that Julie got offered a job at the orthopedic center. I knew that she was leaving but we both never talked about it. She never mentioned anything and continued to work as if nothing had happened. In my heart I was in denial and did not have the courage to face the reality. Two weeks later after getting her paycheck she left and never came back. I was really devastated.

Darlene was still coming to the office of and on just to chat with me. Through her I found out how Julie was doing. Darlene informed me that she was working for an orthopedic surgeon who was giving her more money than me.

A few months later I found out that Julie had filed a lawsuit against the same surgeon for sexual harassments. By then Julie had been diagnosed to have breast cancer. She underwent bilateral mastectomy. She lost her job and had no finances to pay for her illness. Her live-in boyfriend had a new girlfriend. Her kids were in college on full soccer scholarship. Her son was in UNC and daughter was playing for Duke. Her older daughter had run away from home 16 weeks pregnant to an unknown city. All of this was told to me when Julie had been deceased for about 2 years.
We had hired a third person as it would make the office run more efficiently as per Julie's recommendation. I knew why she was insisting

on that because she had plans to leave. Even till today, I do not know why I did not stop her from leaving me. I had always known that nobody could replace her. Her death was shocking to everyone who knew her.

Kathy was hired by Julie. Vivian, Julie and Kathy would have made a very good team if it had lasted. After Julie left Kathy almost took over the whole show. She made many changes in the office, of course with my permission. Each chart was color coded and had labels for whatever was in it. She also scheduled patients very differently. I had stopped going to Cushing as I was very busy in my office. I started doing EMG's all day on Wednesdays in the office instead of going to outreach Clinics. I was very pleased with the schedule changes.

Kathy was in her late thirties and had one young son. She informed me that her father was a very famous thoracic surgeon. She also told me that she had four sisters. Two of her sisters graduated from Holland Hall, a very well-known private school, and the other two went to Jenks public school. Her son also went to Holland Hall. She was divorced to which she had adjusted very well. She was very pleasant to work with.

She would bring snacks to the office several times a week and would be very excited for all special occasions. For example, Valentine's Day she would bring homemade cookies along with small gifts for everyone. On my birthday when I walked into my office I saw a cake, big bouquet of flowers and several expensive gifts. I knew the store where she got them from as it was well known for its unique gifts.

This exchange of gifts continued almost throughout the year

She would sometime take a few hours off to go to Holland Hall school for meetings. I knew about these meetings because my children went to the same school. She also informed me that she had cordial relationship with her ex-husband. Her son sometimes would go and spend several weeks with him at a time. She told me where her father's house was. I knew that house as I usually drove by it to go home. It was a mansion in one of the expensive neighborhoods

She showed me pictures of her sisters celebrating their mother's birthday in their lake house. That lake house itself looked very pretty. There was also a picture of a big yacht outside their lake house. She presented as a rich girl brought up with good family values. She often mentioned going to operation theater with her father. It did not sound right but I didn't know what surgeons can do to train their children. She said that she was training to be a surgical technician so was allowed to go to operation theater. I knew of Dr. White but had not met him yet in person.

I found it somewhat odd when she would flirt with some of the young drug reps. who would come to the office. She always mentioned that she would like to date someone younger than her and have another child.

Within a few weeks, a first-grade teacher of Holland Hall, who was my patient came to the office and I introduced her to Kathy. I mentioned that two of her sisters had been students at the school where she had taught. On her next visit she informed me that they had never had any students by names that Kathy gave for her sisters. I did not pay much attention to this. I asked my children if they had heard of these girls who would have been a few years senior to them. My kids also had never heard of anyone by that first or last name in their school.

Kathy had impressed me so much that I ignored all this thinking that these girls might have been in different classes and not very well known to my kids.

§ * – DID I?

One day I realized that I had lost or misplaced my debit card. So, I called the bank. They informed me that they would mail me a replacement card and a new security code in separate envelopes. It so happened that I was supposed to go to India the same month. I told Kathy that while I'm gone there will be some envelopes coming from the bank and she should just lock them to which she said yes.

By this time, we had Vivian and Kathy working in the office and work was going relatively smoothly. Vivian told me that she would like to take about a week off while I was gone. I came back after a month and started working. The office was always very busy whenever I would come back from vacations. I checked my mail within next couple of days. When I was looking into my bank statements, I noticed that while I was in India $5,000 had been withdrawn from my checking account. I called the bank, and they verified the ATM location from where the money was taken out. I informed them that I was in India and there was no way I could have withdrawn money from an ATM location in Oklahoma. The bank had a picture of the person who did it. I did not know that a picture is taken when you're making transactions. I went to the bank and saw the picture of the person who had withdrawn the money. I could see that it was a Caucasian male who was totally bald. I had no recollection of knowing any person like that. The bank informed me that while the investigations were going on they would put the money back in my account and I would not be penalized for it. I, at that time realized that while I was gone, my ATM card and security code came and both envelopes had been opened. I did not say anything about it because the girls in the office usually opened everything and brought it to me every day. The ones that were labeled confidential and personal were left on my desk unopened. I did mention to Kathy what had happened and how somebody had withdrawn $5,000 from my account. I showed her the picture. Her response was astonishing. She said and I quote "if somebody is stealing money, he or she will not take the card and withdraw the money themselves". She said that you can easily pay someone 20 dollars and ask them to withdraw money for you. I asked who those people were who would be willing to commit a crime like that. She mentioned so many categories of people who she knew had done it and would be willing to do it. I was shocked. I had always had a soft corner for people who are homeless and financially compromised. I did not know that they were being used for these kinds of fraudulent activities by certain kind of people. I thought that may be Kathy had something to do with this act but I didn't have a proof so I couldn't take an action.

By now Kathy was dating a young man who was barely 20. He would sometimes bring lunch for her and on several occasions would come in the evening to pick her up. After about six months Kathy announced that she was pregnant with child of this young man. Kathy decided that she would not work during the latter part of her pregnancy. She would return to work three months after delivery. She left in the last month of her pregnancy. It was a friendly departure, and my assumption was that she would be back after childbirth. I later came to know that she did not work for several months. By then her position had been filled in my office. About a year later she went to work for another neurologist in town who happened to be a good friend of mine. She called me a few months later and during the conversation casually mentioned that DR. White's daughter was working for her. She had nothing but admiration for this girl. She also knew that Kathy had worked for me previously.

Dr. White joined Hillcrest Hospital about two years after Kathy had left me. By then she had also left the other neurologist's employment. I became very friendly with Dr. White and his nurse. We would often have lunch together in doctor's dining room. During one of these luncheons, I told Dr. White that his daughter Kathy had worked for me. He was surprised and told me immediately that he did not have a daughter by the name of Kathy. Then I told him the whole story. He was completely taken aback. He wanted to see a picture of Kathy and know every detail about her. I unfortunately did not have any pictures of Kathy when she was employed at my office. I told Dr. White about the other neurologist where she had been employed and told the same story. He got in touch with the other neurologist who apparently was told the same stories as me. Dr. White got in touch with the police and informed me months later that this girl was an imposter. The first and the last name she used were all fake. She even used fake I/D for everything. The police were still tracing her when Dr. White left and moved to another hospital. I lost touch and didn't pursue this matter.

In my office we had hired Ashley who was in her late 20's. She was married do a young man who was a driver and worked for EMSA. They were so much in love. He would honk three times whenever he was close to our office building. This was his way of letting her know that he was nearby. She came from a very educated family and aspired to be a physician. She was an excellent worker. She started taking classes for pre-med. She enrolled one course at a time and finished it at her own pace She had an aunt who had done the same thing and took five years to finish all courses to go to medical school. She became a successful practitioner years later at Saint John's Hospital.

Alicia did extremely well in the office and took over typing and many responsibilities from Vivian. She became pregnant 3 times during her employment and each time after a month she would come back and work even better than before. Her having small children and being so efficient was very impressive. She never stopped going to school and always made A grade in all her classes. Soon I found out that she had started having problems with her husband. He did not progress in his carrier and had no desire to do anything other than being a driver. Ashley left her employment and moved to California to be close to her parents. She divorced her husband couple of years later. Her father was a physician who supported her till she finished medical school.

Before Alicia left, she managed to find a mature Lady by the name of Doris for our office. Bonita again came from Houston to help in finalizing the recruitment. Doris had been a waitress for many years. She was educated and wanted to work in a medical field. She turned out to be very good worker. Even though she did not have experience working in an office setting she still managed to please everybody. She had good mannerism and excellent work ethics. She was very punctual and was eager to learn. Vivian by this time had been with us for almost five yrs. Bonita had been billing and managing the practice for 12 yrs. She trained Doris with patience. Things were going smoothly. Doris spoke to patients with a smile and addressed them as darling. honey. baby etc. Soon we realized that this was not enough, so we let her go within her three-month probation period.

Bonita again came to my rescue and helped me hire Kendra. When Kendra came for an interview, she appeared prefect for the job... She had Bachelor's in science degree and had worked in many different clinics as per her resume. She was last employed in an outpatient Psychiatry Clinic in Sapulpa. She was of Asian descent but proficient in English. The day I interviewed her she was dressed in a high-neck full sleeve shirt and had a blazer on. She looked very presentable. I soon found out that her previous employment was in the same clinic where one of my psychiatrist friends was working. I called her to get a reference but could not connect. I liked Kendra so much that I offered her the job the same day and asked her to start the next day. She practically took over the office and gave no one any reason to complaint. She was required to wear scrubs in the office. It took her about two weeks to buy scrubs. She was waiting to get her paycheck till then. The very first day when she came to the office in scrubs it was obvious that she had tattoos all over her body including the neck. I didn't say anything but politely asked her to wear something with full sleeves. She managed to wear a scarf around her neck so her tattoos will not show either.

My psychiatrist friend had gone out of town for two weeks. She called me soon after she got back. I wanted to know about Kendra although it didn't matter as she had already been hired. I was totally shocked to hear the information she provided. She told me that Kendra used to live in New York before moving to Oklahoma. Apparently, she was involved in a gang murder case and was wanted by the police in New York. She became a fugitive & moved to Sapulpa about six months ago. She also had a small child that she brought with her. The police came looking for her in Sapulpa but fortunately for her she was not working that day. The next day when she came to work, she was told about it. She made up an excuse about an unpaid driving ticket for which the police might be after her and continued to work till the end of the day. She didn't come to work after that day. A few weeks later she applied for the job at our office. I was informed that the police were still looking for her actively. I was also told that she had used many different names previously. I asked Bonita to call her after hours and told her that she did not have to return to work the next day. She did not ask any questions. I felt as though she was expecting this phone call. I never heard from the police or from anyone asking about her. Fortunately, she had already been paid for the number of hours she had worked. I never judged her for her tattoos. Instead, she was complemented about her skills many times during the time she was employed at our clinic.

Vivian was again handling the office all by herself. Next week a patient of mine from Cushing, during her visit, asked me if I would help her daughter find a job. She had just graduated from OSU with a bachelor's degree. This patient had adopted this girl from Mexico when she was just a baby as she herself was unable to have children. She raised her all by herself after her husband passed away. Her daughter graduated from college and was looking for a job in medical field. She was 23 years old. I had seen her a few times when she came to the office with her mother. We hired Tina and had no problem training her. At the suggestion of Bonita, we also hired Dominique as enough was enough and I was not going to let Vivian be by herself under any circumstances. Tina took over the typing and a lot of front office work. Dominique would make appointments and help Vivian with checking in and out of the new patients.

Tina lived in Cushing. She drove every morning for an hour and 15 minutes and was never late. She left exactly at 5pm and never complained about the distance. Her mother called to thank me for hiring her daughter. Our pay days have always been 1st and 16th of each month. Tina was hired on first of that month. This was her first paycheck as she had never worked before. She finished college in three years as she went to school even during the summertime, she had never actually had a job prior to this. After getting her paycheck she literally came and hugged me and thanked me again. It was Friday around 5pm when she left to drive home. At around 6pm that evening I got a call from the police that one of my employees was in an accident. Apparently when Kendra was driving to Cushing, she changed the lane and had a head-on collision. She died on the spot. Her family was informed and because there was a telephone number for my office on the paycheck, I was also called. The police informed me that her body would be taken to a funeral home after completion of the autopsy. I called her mother to express my grief over the loss of this young bright girl.

For the viewing a few days later I along with my husband went to Cushing. I was surprised to find out that Kendra was married. Her husband was a maintenance worker at OSU. Kendra went to OSU on full scholarship, she met this person and married him. He was devastated and her mother could not even talk. The whole family was obviously grief-stricken and shocked. I till this date cannot get over this. This beautiful young enterprising bright girl who worked for me just for 15 days left an impact on me. Her cheerful smiling face after getting her first paycheck was not easy to forget. No matter how much help I offered to her family, no one could bring her back. Her tragic death haunted me for a long time. I kept in touch with her mother for quite some time after this mishap.

In Tulsa and in other cities there were new Hospitals opening for long term acute care of the patients.

I started going to one of them where I eventually became the director of neurology. Patients usually went to these hospitals after acute hospitalization for about 25 days. After those who would become medically stable and capable of enduring comprehensive therapies, they would be transferred to rehab facilities. It was indeed a different experience for me, but I enjoyed it thoroughly. The hospital where I was going with another colleague of mine changed location after a few yrs. It was not convenient for me, so I could not continue. Around same time another one opened where I was invited to provide neurological care by the medical director who had referred patients to me forever. On the very first day. When I was asked to see eight consultations for him in the hospital a situation happened which I cannot forget. There was another neurologist who used to see consultations at this hospital. Apparently, the administration was not very pleased with him and wanted him to leave. I was not aware of it. When my colleague asked me to see eight patients that were previously seen by the other neurologist, it became very awkward. He cornered me and threatened me that if I ever go near any of these patients It would be very detrimental to me. I immediately reported this incident to my colleague and to the hospital administration. By that evening that doctor was escorted out of the hospital by security. He was never allowed back in or around the hospital building. I have never had this kind of experience as a physician. After a few months I ran into that physician at another hospital. He stopped and apologized for his behavior. He told me about his recent divorce, money issues, custody battles and several lawsuits without mentioning details. I felt very sorry for him and understood what he was going through.

This hospital became a significant part of part of my practice and I'm still working there after so many years. I have seen many ups and downs. The hospital has been bought and sold several times with name changes as well. I became very interested in this kind of enterprise. Once I took it upon myself to go to Arkansas, to a facility where patients with traumatic brain injury were treated. My husband came along with me, and we spent a whole day there. I got to see the mechanics of this facility and learned a lot. That facility in Arkansas was a hidden treasure. Patients were admitted with traumatic brain injury and after staying there for three to six months, went home with much less disability.

I was lucky to be involved in the care of some of the traumatic brain injury and motor vehicle accident patients at the facility in Tulsa. One of the patients was a young man. He was out on a motorcycle with his girlfriend when the accident happened. Patient became totally unresponsive and had a very pronged Illness. His family came from out of town and stayed with him. His girlfriend was initially visiting him quite often, but later she stopped coming completely. His parents were living in a room that her son had occupied while he was a student at the local university. His parents came in a hurry and did not bring enough personal need items or clothes. They did not know that they would have to stay in Tulsa for several months. I noticed that his father was wearing same clothes every day. Of course, I never. mentioned anything to them about this but asked if I could bring him. anything. To my surprise, the first thing that he asked for me to bring was shirts, trousers and possibly shoes. Luckily, he had almost the same size as my husband. So, I brought him enough clothes as soon as I could. The family was very thankful to me. Every time patient's father would wear clothes, brought by me he would give me a peculiar smile. I asked him never to mention about it to anyone. Luckily, the patient recovered enough so he could be transferred to a rehab facility in Colorado. After a prolonged stay there he recovered to the extent that he was able to talk and walk with some assistance. These kinds of experiences make a physician want to continue to work forever and ever.

Again, I will come back to my office staff because they facilitated and helped this family in many ways to make their stay in Tulsa comfortable. We always worked as a team and took pride in doing so.

Coming back to the office Vivian and Dominique worked together very well. Bonita continued to supervise remotely. By this time, we had also started to accept externs from local trade Colleges. The girls who were trying to be front office assistant or medical assistant had to do 6 weeks of internship in a doctor's office. Vivian would interview them and help these young girls so they could be front office workers. We hired some of these girls and gave them full-time jobs for next several years.

I met Heather, who was a unit secretary at a hospital. She was barely 19 and had just met her boyfriend. She decided she did not want to work the evenings or weekends but wanted to continue in the medical field. She had indicated several times that she would like to come and work for me. I already had three girls in the office and was not looking for any additional help. Vivian unfortunately slipped on ice and strained her back. She took almost a month off because she had difficulty walking. Dominique along with the extern was suddenly given responsibility of running the office. Bonita came to my rescue and started helping more than before even though it was a remote operation. I took two weeks off around the holidays at the end of the year and went out of country. There was always a neurologist covering for me. We often had to take care of lot of patient related stuff during office hours. Even in my absence, I kept in touch via telephone calls and email. My trip had been planned almost a year ago. Dominique and the intern were supposed to be in the office. In my absence, Dominique had to take time off because she had some personal issues. The only person left in the office was the intern. She knew nothing about the office. I would have flown back but since I was out of country, it was not possible. Bonita assured me that the intern will manage the daily affairs under her supervision for two days which was also her last day with us. Vivian was supposed to come back in the second week. Dominique came back the next day which was a big relief for me. In my absence Dominique figured out a trick she would forward office calls to her cell phone and not show up in the office. She would answer phone calls remotely and act as if she was in the office. when I came back from my vacation the mailman informed me that he had to leave my mail on several days' downstairs with the property manager. She managed to even fool Bonita in Houston. This was shocking to me as I had never had this happen in my absence before. Fortunately, the patients did not have problem as the physician who was covering for me took care of them. Dominique would be referring most of patient's related issues to the covering physician who took care of everything and never complained.

Vivian came back and started working just like before. With mutual consent we decided to let Dominique go and hire Heather from Specialty Hospital. Heather had quit her job and was sitting at home. She was very happy to come and work for me. She again showed her skills and became a part of the team within a few weeks.

Vivian turned 55 and started to indicate she wanted to retire. Her children did not want her to work full time. She had started having back pain which was persisting more than before.

I thought Heather would last a long time with me as she was just 20 years old. She worked hard and impressed me a lot. After 6 months of employment, she came and informed me that she was engaged do her boyfriend whom she had been dating for a while.

She was very excited about the upcoming wedding. She collected precious dolls merchandise. She wanted cake and decorations to look like various dolls that she had collected over the years. She had started getting sick and would often complain of being tired. She soon found out that she was pregnant. All hell broke loose after that. She became very emotional and would cry at the drop of the hat. She would become aggressive to the extent that sometimes I had to ask her to be in a room by herself. Her personality changed totally during pregnancy. She started taking time off to go to the doctor quite often. She was even referred to a psychiatrist. I had never seen a person becoming like this just because they're pregnant. I later found out that there was a lot going on in her family and between her and her fiancé. There was also a possibility that the wedding might have to be postponed or even cancelled When she was about seven months pregnant, she could not even come to work because she had gained a lot of weight and her mental condition was unstable. She was prescribed various medications and was asked to rest at home.

Vivian again came through for me and started to recruit office help. We hired Linda who had lot of experience in this field. Her ex-husband was a general surgeon at the hospital where I worked. I knew him very well. She was very pleasant and disciplined. She did not have to be trained more than a few days. She appeared to be very knowledgeable and professional. She got along very well with Vivian. The office was again running smoothly, the billing was being done by Bonita. I was sending her the billing information every week without any delay.

Linda did not have any children. Over the next few months, it became clear the reasons she took up this job as our office close to the hospital where her ex worked. She always knew his schedule as to when he was operating and when he would be taking a lunch break. She would schedule her breaks around his schedule. None of us knew about all this until she herself told Vivian everything. Unfortunately, she was not allowed to be near her ex-husband legally as he had filed restraining orders against her, she had a depressive personality for which she compensated by laughing excessively. She lasted for a couple of years and eventually got frustrated as her mission was not successful. She finally moved out of Oklahoma to be close to her elderly parents.

§ * – WHICH TAB IS OPEN IN MY MIND

We hired a young girl named Karen. She was raised by her grandparents who lived in Sapulpa. She was very shy and hardly spoke all day. This was her first job as a front office clerk. She had worked as a medical assistant in another office previously. She was very punctual and methodical. Vivian took her under her wings and groomed her very well.

I soon had to replace Vivian with Camilla when she decided to retire. Camilla had been an office manager at another doctor's office. She was very authoritative and aggressive. She had the qualities of being an office manager and a leader.

Camilla daily came from home to work and then went back home. She did not appear to be very social. As per information that she gave us she was mostly homebound after work and in the weekends. I went on vacation to Arizona and asked Camilla to interview a few candidates for the job of an EEG technician in the office. Camilla had also taken a week off during that time. I thought that she would finish interviewing the three candidates in one day but when I came back, I was told that Camilla came daily for 8 hours and interviewed candidates. There were only three applicants, but she spent 40 hours interviewing them. The final decision was that none of them was worth it. I thought it was very odd. Karen told me that Camilla come to the office and sat in my office for couple of hours while I was gone. The girls would be interviewed and leave within 30 minutes. The total time spent was no more than couple of hours. I still let Camilla work because of the good qualities she had and never mentioned anything about this incident.

Karen was still very quiet and docile. She started to complain of dizziness and weakness. She soon informed us that she was pregnant. She was dating a Hispanic guy who lived in Kansas City and came to Oklahoma only occasionally. When he found out about the pregnancy, he was very supportive. He apparently rented an apartment for her and started to support her financially. After her delivery she took about three months off. She came back to work as her grandmother was taking care of the baby. She never got married and did not see her boyfriend much. He however continued to support her and the baby financially.

Camila on the other hand was being awkward many a times. We used to have an old-fashioned EEG machine which required lot of ink. I had to order ink every 4 to 6 months. The digital EEG machine was bought a few years later. I went for a meeting to Dallas for couple of days and in my absence six large bottles of ink were delivered. When I came back, I was told the ink never arrived. I called the company, and they showed me signature of person who received the shipment. The signature was not legible. I ordered the ink again and business continued as usual. Later, I found out that this ink was used to manufacture methamphetamine and it might have reached wrong hands before or after delivery. I did not have any proof, so I dismissed this incident and continued with my work. There were also few occasions when the money that was collected at the window was not deposited in the bank. It was Bonita who finally found out that Camilla was mishandling the window collection and had to go. Bonita helped me hire Mary and let Camilla go.

Mary had moved to Oklahoma from Hawaii 7 years ago. She had worked in a doctor's office for about 6 months in the past. She always had a smile on her face and wore a flower over her right ear as traditionally the Hawaiians do. I thought it was cute. She was friendly to the patients and always greeted them with open arms She almost became a leader in the office.

Couple of months after starting this job Mary took a few days off to go to Las Vegas for a reunion. Several times a day from Las Vegas she would call to see how office work was going. She let me know that she would make sure that the office goes on smoothly even in her absence. She also spoke to Camilla several times.

I only knew that she had experience working in a doctor's office and that she was from Hawaii. I started noticing that daily around 4pm a lady would come and sit in the waiting room. I was informed she was there to take Mary home. Sometimes our patients would still be there when Hora who was Mary's ride would arrive. Mary would continue to work till it was time to go. Mary would often refer to Hora as her ride. Mary had lost custody of her daughters who were living with their father. So much so that due to legal issues she was not even allowed to speak to her daughters who were teenagers. When she moved to Tulsa, she had nowhere to go. She met Hora at a grocery store. She took her to her apartment and supported her for several months till

Mary could find a job. They have since been living together. She would refer to Hora as her partner.

After about a year I saw a change in Mary's behavior. She would wake up in the morning and call me in a very slurred slow monotonous voice that she was not feeling well and could not come to work. The very next day she would be at work smiling and very cheerful as she always was. This happened several times in the next six months to follow. But this time Karen's boyfriend asked her to move in with him in Kansas City with their baby, so she decided to leave. Before Karen left, we hired Ellen who had been working with us as an extern. Ellen was very familiar with our office. She was hired on Thursday and the next day on Friday Lisa did not show up. She called in a very sultry voice to inform me that she will not show up. I was very upset that she left a girl, who had barely started in the office about 24 hours ago, all to herself to manage the full schedule. Mary came to the office that day to help. She was not herself. She appeared as though she was drunk but I could not smell any alcohol on her. I still appreciated the fact that she came to finish the job.

We were getting very busy in the office and could not survive with one new girl and Mary who had started to take more time off than usual. We hired another secretary for the front office by the name of Emma. Bonita was billing efficiently or so I thought, and I was working hard at the office and a hospital. Practice was going well.

It almost became a habit with Mary to call in sick and then show up the next day. I had learned my lesson and never questioned her and let her continue with this behavior. I had steady help in the office so there was not much disruption when she was absent.

We have a medicine cabinet in our office where the samples are kept locked. The key to this cabinets is usually with the front office assistants.

It was brought to my attention that we were missing sample of Soma, a muscle relaxant which is very addictive. We never used to get any samples for Soma, but the company came up with a newer version and started sampling it for a few months. I have never been very fond of dispensing Soma. I did think the slurred speech with which Mary would call every so often could be as a result of her taking Soma but I never saw her steal the medication and or take it so I could not question her about it.

Mary had been with me for more than two years. Most of the patients liked her and she was always willing to please me. She would go out with some of the guys who worked in the building. She would tell the other girls in the office about it the next day. We hired Emma to help Mary

Mary had started to be very social and outgoing. I also started suspecting that medication cabinet was not being handled properly. One day Mary indicated that she wanted to go back to Hawaii as she was going to get custody of her daughters. She resigned and I accepted her resignation. She came to the office and give her badge back to me and left. I never questioned her about mishandling of medication sample or anything else.

While she was away presumably in Hawaii one day, I got a call from a detective who informed me that somebody from my office was calling in a prescription for Norco, a potent narcotic, every two weeks. The person who was calling the prescription would put on an accent trying to mimic me and call in a prescription for 150 tablets at a time. Most of the pharmacist in town knew that I did not prescribe narcotics in that large quantity. The detective questioned me if I was prescribing the medications to a patient by the name of Mary. I, of course denied it immediately. I suspected that Mary might be doing it, but I didn't have a proof. Pharmacists at this store knew me. One day the detective informed me that Norco prescription was called again, and Mary was supposed to pick it up that evening. Apparently, Mary's partner drove her to the Drive-In Pharmacy. Mary presented her driver's license while seated in the passenger seat. The pharmacist dispensed the medication and as soon as she picked it up, she was apprehended. Detectives called me immediately and asked me to go there to witness this, but I didn't want to do that. Mary was imprisoned for three years after several court proceedings. I was completely out of the picture during all of this. A few years later, after getting out of prison, Mary called me to request if I'd hire her back.

One of my EEG technicians named Marion knew how to follow a person while they were in prison. She would keep me posted about the whole case till she got out. She called me a few months later to see if I would hire her back. I knew not to make that kind of mistake again.

I hired Ginger who was previously employed as an EEG technician at Hillcrest. She retired from hillcrest and came to work for me. She was already doing EEGs in my office on regular bases on her days off. I asked her to help me with the front office also. Ginger was always very kind and respectful to me besides being an excellent technician. We got along very well. She did not want to work full-time because she was not feeling well due to some abdominal pain that she had been experiencing. She informed me that gastroenterologist had told her that she needed surgery for pancreatic problem. She would not eat and soon lost a lot of weight. I suspected ginger had pancreatic cancer. I never wanted to mention about it. I offered to help her in every which way possible. She however continued to be secretive about her illness. She could not continue to work at my office as she got very sick. She had already hired another EEG technician to fill in for her. It was then she told me that she was battling pancreatic cancer. She died a few months later. During her illness we kept in touch. She never asked for any help from any one of us. A few years before her passing her brother had moved in with her. It was through him that we could communicate. I went for the viewing of her body to say goodbye to her after her death.

One of my patients who was also Ginger's best friend informed me about Ginger's personal life which was very intricate. Ginger had been divorced for a very long time. She raised her only son as a single mother. He unfortunately died at a very young age. She became depressed and stayed isolated for a long time. She always appeared very normal at work to me. A few months later she told her best friend that she had a boyfriend who was Hispanic living in Texas. They would talk to each other for hours every night. This had been going on for several months. She never visited him in Texas. She would often show jewelry that she received from her boyfriend. After her death her friend found out that she didn't have a boyfriend. She bought jewelry with her own money to show others. Her brother who was living with her for a long time told her friend that Ginger went to bed very early even when she was not sick. Her brother found several boxes of jewelry in her room after her death. He sent me a couple of pairs of earnings as memorabilia. Her sisters didn't know of her having a boyfriend either. She will always be a good friend in my heart. A nice person who helped me tremendously. I miss her immensely even now.

It also reminds me of an incidence involving another patient. I was taking care of her at one of the hospitals where I worked, when she passed. I would often visit with her son while she was alive. He was a jewelry designer by profession. A few weeks After her death he showed up at my office and presented me a gift box. He informed me that he had designed a pendent specially for me. I gladly accepted It. It was a beautiful pendent. I thanked him and opened the box when he was about to leave. The pendent had beautiful colored stones. He informed me that those were her deceased mother's teeth which he had carved into different shapes and painted them. I almost fainted looking at that gift but couldn't say anything to him.

While Ginger was working at Hillcrest, she needed help in performing EEG. Hillcrest sent an employee by the name of Jack, who was a Monitor tech, to be trained as an EEG technician. Ginger started him from scratch and made him an expert in this technology. He started to perform EEGs for Hillcrest patients as Ginger's assistant. He would sometimes come to the office with Ginger, so we all knew him. After Ginger passed, I hired Jack. who by then had left Hillcrest and was unemployed? Jack was indeed a good technician. He did the job very well. He, however, had too many personal issues about which I had no knowledge. He. worked two days a week. He would always come on time. After a few months he asked if he could do the EEEs one day a week and on Saturdays. I agreed not knowing the reason why he wanted to do this. He was performing his duty and there was no problem with the EEGs. One day he cancelled all the patients that had been scheduled on a Wednesday. When I spoke to him the next day he came to the clinic, he informed me that he had four children under the age of five and his current wife had taken up a job. So, during weekdays, he had to take care of his children That. opened a Pandora's box. I came to know that he had eight children with four different women. All the women who had been in his life were suing him for child support. His current wife was in trouble with the law and was imprisoned leaving him with the kids. I felt very sorry for him and decided to work with his schedule and not fire him. I did, however, hire another technician to come during weekdays and gave him Saturdays. He continued to have monetary problems and lost his car. On couple of occasions, I personally had to go and bring him from his residence to the clinic.

Emma had started working for us after Mary left. Even when I had started having problem with Mary's frequent absentees, Emma would often bring a friend of her to help when needed. New era began in my office when Emma 's friend Edith joined us. She had been working at dish TV for the past few months. She was also trying to finish college online. It almost appeared like Emma was bossing over Edith which she did not like. I admire the fact that despite this kind of hostility Edith learned everything from her and became as efficient as Emma was. Emma was living with her boyfriend and had a young daughter. Her boyfriend was not very supportive of her daughter, so the relationship was not going well. They had signed a lease together for an apartment and were therefore living under the same roof. They separated after the lease was finished. Emma also moved out of town to be close to her mother who offered to take care of her daughter.

Edith had already mastered everything about Botox authorizations from Emma. We had been recognized in Tulsa for providing Botox therapy for various neurological conditions. The very first day that she was hired she informed me that she was going through a divorce and that would be finalized in the next few months. Her ex-husband was very angry with her. In the divorce decree he had put down a clause which prevented her from using her married name. Edith came from broken home and did not talk much about her parents. As a worker she was excellent. She started several new things in the office which were very helpful. She was also taking care of an elderly lady in the morning before coming to work. Soon she started dating a young man and suddenly her personality changed. She would dress better and became even more efficient. After about six months of employment, she informed me that her boyfriend was in prison for a few months for minor offence. During this time, she became somewhat sad but not for long as she had several girlfriends to support her. Edith had already met someone, and the relationship was going very well to the extent she started thinking about marriage. She even asked me if I would give her away at the time of her wedding, I thought it was an honor therefore I gladly agreed.

Edith came on time and worked very efficiently. I had no complaints about her work. She knew how to be a leader she was very professional with the patients and a good teacher for the externs that came to us for training.

After Emma left, we decided to hire a friend of Edith who had worked previously with her. Her name was Mary, and she was a close friend of Edith. She was very polite and indeed very efficient. Things were going smoothly in the office, but the personal life of Mary was in a turmoil. Edith was not getting along with her current boyfriend. She also had problems with his ex-wife. Edith never let her personal life affect her work. Mary was calm and quiet. She was living with her elderly boyfriend and was trying very hard to get pregnant. Unfortunately, in the next four to six months Mary had two miscarriages which made her very sad and depressed. Around the same time, Edith broke up with her boyfriend as he refused to marry her. Soon she came to know that her previous boyfriend was getting out of prison which made her very excited. When he was released, they got back together happily. He was very fatherly to her then teenage boys. Apparently, he went back to his old job and even helped the boys to get the part time job with him. In a few months she found out that her current boyfriend who was living with her had also been pursuing his ex-girlfriend with whom he had a child. Their relationship went sour again. Edith asked him to move out and became single once again.

Mary after having had two miscarriages became pregnant and decided to stay at home during pregnancy as advised by her doctor. We were again left with only one person in the office but only for a day. Edith called a friend of hers named Jennifer who was also trained and was looking for a job. I was desperate so, I hired her. She had a very childlike behavior which was intolerable. She had to be told what to do and once she got the hang of it, she was able to perform well. She was also in a relationship which was not going very well. She would sit in the office and cry at her desk. Edith and Jennifer hung out with same group of people. One of their friends suddenly died of drug overdose They both wanted to go for the funeral which means the office would have to be closed. Edith suggested that one person can go for viewing of the body and the other one could go for the funeral. I thought this was a good suggestion and I agreed. Edith went for viewing of the body and only had to leave an hour early as it was in the evening. On the day of funeral Jennifer was very upset and wanted Edith to go with her. She almost had a nervous breakdown when Edith refused. They all knew that I was going to California frequently to see my sick mother. Jennifer came to my office, slammed the door and said some very intimidating things about my mother. I was shocked. Edith acted responsibly and immediately asked Jennifer to leave the office. I never heard from her again. We never discussed about this incident. On the contrary we hired yet another friend of Edith within couple of days. Again, a very well-trained polite woman by the name of Gia. Edith made sure that everything was done properly. Work started to go smoothly again.

Edith had started to date a different person. She was going out almost evening. She still worked very efficiently. Gia also had a story regarding her lifestyle. She had a child from a previous relationship who was 5 years old and was living with his father. Gia wanted to get custody but was not able to do so as she did not have a place to live or a job. It was perhaps one of the reasons that she came to work for us very gladly which was a blessing for us. In next few months Gia got into a relationship with a well-established guy who had a five-year-old son. Gia was a good mother and took very good care of this young boy. She was often sad and confused that she's putting all her efforts in raising her boyfriend's son while her own child was living far away from her. She could never even see him due to legal issues. She was able to reunite with her son eventually. She chose to live in the same town as he did. This was ordered by the judge.

One day the news came that Edith's ex-husband was hospitalized after having been shot. Luckily, he survived. He was in the hospital for a long time. Edith took good care of her ex and slept every evening in the hospital. Despite all this she came to work every morning on time, finished her job and even took care of kids efficiently.

Edith had a habit of announcing to everyone when it was close to her birthday. All the patients knew that her birthday was coming. Most of the drug reps were made aware that her birthday was approaching fast. Even some of our patients knew that Edith was going to have a birthday soon. I almost treated her like my younger sister. When we were growing up my mother would not just celebrate our birthday but would always celebrate our birthday month. Which means that right from the beginning of the month till the end, my mother would give us a gift if not every day but at least several times a week. These were small gifts which kids usually adore. For that month my siblings and I were made to feel like real prince and princesses. I had that feeling with Edith. We were getting along well so, when she announced that her birthday was coming, I told her that I would celebrate her birthday week. I am glad I did that.

§ * – CAN'T BE YOUR SUPPLY

Almost every Friday would be our Botox clinic. Botox would be delivered to the office and refrigerated. I always knew how much Botox was there in the office. One day while we were talking to each other during our free time, Edith told me that she and her friends went for a Botox party. Apparently, a nurse was providing cosmetic Botox. The nurse usually brought Botox from the office where she worked. I decided that I would take Botox home and bring it to our office whenever it would be time to inject. That is continuing still. Botox can be deadly in wrong hands.

Lily and Edith worked out a good plan. Lily's job was checking patients in and out, preparing charts and calling in prescriptions. Edith did everything else. She called herself specialist in dealing with patients who needed Botox therapy. She was a good typist. multitasker and had good interpersonal relationship with the staff and patients. Her ex-husband was released from the hospital but became disabled as he was unable to work So he didn't have to pay child support any more. Edith always had two jobs to be able to take care of her children. She had stopped looking for a boyfriend and was concentrating more on her children. She also groomed Lily very well in our office.

One day while I was in my office one of my secretaries informed me that there was a physician in the waiting room wanting to visit with me. Even though I was busy I decided to spend a few minutes with him. To my utter surprise I saw Dr Y, sitting in the waiting room. I invited him in. I was very surprised to see him looking so different. To my surprise the doctor came in a trench coat, shabby outfit, dirty shoes and ungroomed hair. At first, I could not understand why he was at my office. He would have called me or made an appointment if he needed neurological care. He was very well known to me as a Hillcrest ER physician. He stood right in front of me and asked me to write a prescription for a controlled substance for him without making any conversation. I however, despite my surprise, kept my cool and refused. He did not want to budge and continued to request repeatedly. He said that he was in pain and needed it urgently. He also said that he would not come back again. While I was talking to him there was a phone call for me from another doctor who had an office in the same building. I was told that it was urgent, so I excused myself and spoke to her. She had called to let me know that this doctor was going to different doctor's offices looking for drugs. He was high on some substances that he had used and looked like he had not slept for a long time. I was calm but somewhat scared of him. I continued to talk and at the same time pressed the panic button. Security officers came and escorted him out of my office within minutes. At that time, I was told that he is heavily into drugs and had exhibited inappropriate behavior at work. His license to practice had been suspended.

This was an eye opener for me that I should not allow anyone in the office without knowing the reason why they are there

Edith was very affectionate towards the patients. She would bring patients the same day if the referring physician thought it was necessary. One day a family physician referred a patient with acute debilitating headaches to be seen urgently. I have a habit of asking too many questions. To the extent that sometimes I interrupt which some of the patients do not appreciate. But that is my way of getting into the history in more details. I am also a trained internist. I have always been proud of the fact that I do not have to refer my patients for most internal medicine problems to other doctors. I do not practice Internal medicine, but I'm very comfortable in diagnosing and treating patients if needed. I even have a habit of listening to their heart and examining the breast and abdomen etc. I guess old habits die hard. While I was examining this patient, I felt a very hard lump in her breast. When I questioned her. She told me that yes, she had noticed it, but she was not paying any attention to it because sometimes it would get soft. To cut the long story short, this patient was sent for further testing and was found to have carcinoma of the breast stage four, which had metastasized to her brain and that was one of the reasons for her severe headaches. Ignorance is a bliss. But in this case, it was deadly.

I was assigned a parking spot in the hospital parking lot with my name written on it which was very convenient. Sometimes I would come very early so I could finish rounding at the hospital on time especially when I was on call. I noticed that in the mornings that the whole parking lot was empty, except for one red car. I saw that car parked in the same spot all day perhaps all night because it never moved. I did not know who that car belonged to. I became curious to find out as the parking spot was only two cars down from my spot. I soon found out that it belonged to another doctor in the same building who was purposely parking it at a spot where there was no name written. He happened to be a good friend of my husband and I. We often socialized and were invited to many parties at the same time. I then found out that he had problems at home and his wife had kicked him out. He decided to sleep in his office instead of moving into an apartment. He would eat in the hospital cafeteria and then sleep in his office. He informed us himself that he would get dressed early in the morning before his staff arrived. It was a very depressive situation for him. My husband and I and the rest of our friends supported him while he was going through this difficult time. Everything worked out for him after a few months.

Lily was living with a boyfriend. She had three children who were teenagers. Her youngest one was going to school, but the older two boys were neither going to school nor were they working. Her boyfriend was efficient and had a good job. Lily introduced me to her boyfriend who subsequently started to work part-time as a computer consultant for the office. The office proficiency was at its peak with the two of them working hard.

One day Edith came to me and informed me that she had found a teaching job where she would be making more money. She also would be given more benefits. Buy this time I was very dependent on her mainly for Botox. Letting her leave would have meant training a new person which at that time seemed like a big deal. I matched the salary and gave her all the benefits that she asked for and I could afford. She decided to stay and continue to work at the clinic. Lily never raised her voice and was always very pleasant to the patients. She had rough personal life. She couldn't pay her rent or buy a car. She started helping Edith take care of an elderly lady before work. I do not know the details but a few months later, she moved in with her foster sister leaving her children alone. Lily had problems with her family as a teenager She was in college when she became pregnant. Her family denounced her and didn't support her. She began to get close to her classmates' family. They adopted her as one of their own. Lily instead of going home after work would be picked up by a member of this family quite often. She didn't say much about her kids. She was single at that time. Despite having a full-time job Lily was not able to manage her money. Every two weeks when she got her paycheck she would go shopping, buy lunch for everybody in the office and then within a week she would have no money to even buy her own food. She would sometimes eat whatever was available in the office. Edith bought lunch for her several times. I didn't have any idea about this situation till Edith one day informed me. I decided to make sure that every day Lily would have proper lunch. I either brought food for her or gave her money to buy her own lunch. At the end I must mention that more than me Edith helped her. She also often gave her rides to and back from work.

Edith was managing her money very well. She was taking good care of her children as well. Lily failed in all these facets of life for reasons only known to her She went without a reliable transportation for almost 3 years then she decided that she could not take it anymore. She found a man who had a car and decided to live with him. He would bring her to work every morning and pick her up in the evening. Things were going smoothly for a while when after a few months he deserted her and moved out. I offered to give her my old Lexus which was not being used by me or my husband. Lily was very excited at first but then came back and said that this car would be too expensive to repair so she didn't want it. She could've easily sold it and made money, but she did not do that. She wanted to buy a car for a few hundred dollars and asked me to help which I did. Lily could not pay electric bills several times for which she had to ask for help as well.

She had almost reached the end of her rope. She could not pay her electric bill or buy enough groceries. She started going to food pantries to get groceries to feed her adult kids who still were unemployed and totally dependent on their mother. She was given a ride every morning by Edith. They had a difference of opinion on something a few months later and at that time Edith decided not to bring her to work every day. Lily resigned from the job and decided that she would work at a place which was at a walking distance from her apartment. She had enough experience so, she soon got hired by another physician.

Edith again found help and trained her as she did the rest of them. She brought the office back to same level as before and things started to go smoothly. About a year later, she decided to leave me and join another neurologists group. She said that she wanted to work for the person who would be in practice for many more years. We parted on friendly terms. This time I did not want to meet her unreasonable demands like I had done in the past, so I let her go. Before she left, we had already hired another person.

Edith is still missed as a person not because there's any problem in the office. We have started several new things in the office which we are still being followed. We have electronic medical records. This was started by Edith, but I never got into it till I really had to. I went to the office of another physician who had been using it for a long time. We spent a few hours with him and came back with great knowledge about the program that both of us shared. During this time, I also hired the daughter of the same physician's secretary who knew about this program thinking that she will train rest of my girls She lived in Sand Springs and thought it might be too far for her, but she still took the job. She worked very well, and I liked her a lot. She soon became overwhelmed and decided that she did not want to work in doctor's office. She had previously worked as a waitress in a restaurant which she really liked. She got the same job back and left. She liked the hours and the proximity between her residence and the restaurant, so she quit after a few months. She luckily was the third girl in the office, so it did not affect us much.

The drama in the front office however continued. We hired a young girl mainly for record keeping. She needed the job urgently so she could take care of her small infant daughter. She was mainly hired to type which she did very well. She would miss work several times a week because her child was sick and needed medical attention. At the same time, she would post pictures on social media having lunch with her boyfriend and going shopping. This continued for a while and finally she decided not to work. She was already getting help from the government for her child who was well taken care of.

We hired Lana who at the time of interview told us that she was single and had a reliable transport. She worked very well and did not need much training. She later informed the other person in the office that she had two children. They were living with her ex-boyfriend's girlfriend. She didn't have legal custody of her children. She was always staying with so called acquaintances. The whole situation was very complicated. One day she came to me asking for a raise because if she made a certain amount of money every two weeks she would qualify for the apartment.

I gladly gave her a raise in her salary just three months after being hired. I even signed papers recommending her to the prospective company from whom she could rent the apartment. Her behavior was very erratic. On one hand she wanted to make more money and get an apartment to settle down, but at the same time she would misbehave and show mood swings which were not tolerable. She would raise her voice and get mad sometimes at all of us for no apparent reason. I reprimanded her several times and tried to tolerate her because she was a good worker most of the times. After a few weeks she moved on to another job without even giving me her two weeks' notice. She decided not to rent an apartment or seek custody of her children. Fortunately, before she left one of our ex-employees had already expressed desire to come back so the transition went smoothly.

I have spent more than half of my life in this place which I call office. It is my second home. I remember around thanksgiving there used to be a bazar at the hospital where you could buy gifts, jewelry, clothes and many type of gifts. Different vendors would set up booths near the hospital cafeteria. I always liked shopping in these kinds of places. I bought some beautiful necklaces and bracelets from these vendors. I also supported the charities which would also be selling stuff in these kinds of open markets.

The hospital treated us like royalty. Giving us free lunches and inviting us to holiday gala in different hotels. Every year on the second Saturday of December the hospital would have Christmas party. I always bought a new dress for this party and never wore the same one twice. I would go with my husband and meet all the friends. We would try to sit on the same table. We might not be first once to arrive but were always the last once to leave. I remember sitting there with my friends. Some of them were much older than us and some were younger. Age didn't seem to matter. We would just try to look pretty, enjoy good food and dance till late at night.

It was fun to meet spouses of other physicians. After a few years some of them started coming with their new young wives or girlfriends. One of the radiologists sticks out in my memory. he was a neuro radiologist and in my opinion was one of the best ones. He would bring a new lady every time to the party, and it would always be somebody with ethnic features and usually very long hair. I used to think that they were his daughters. A few years later I was informed by other colleagues that they were his girlfriends. He never talked about his children or his family. He was very helpful to me. I often visited him in radiology department to discuss the imaging studies whenever I was in doubt. I admired his radiological acumen and even called him several times for consultations. Our radiology department experienced a drastic change a few years later. Many of the physicians left suddenly. The details were never made public as always.

One of the doctors who left was this neuroradiologist. I heard that he had moved to another city. For many years I never heard anything about him and almost forgot about him. One day, while I was watching a special program about physicians on 60 minutes, to my horror I saw this doctor on the TV. He was filmed by an undercover journalist. He apparently would fly to Columbia to gratify his needs with underage girls. He thought that he was advising another person who had similar interests, but he happened to be an undercover reporter, so everything was videotaped. He was caught red handed talking about the purpose of his recurrent visits to Colombia. It was disgusting to watch it and at the same time I felt sorry for the physician. Such a brilliant physician ruined his life because of certain habits.

§ * – RECOGNITION MATTERS

I feel so elated when I'm recognized wherever I go in this hospital. In the mornings when I enter the building the person who sits at the reception greets me. I usually stop by for a few minutes before going to the hospital for light conversation. The person who sits at the valet parking always comes running to help me if I'm carrying anything to take to the office. When I go to the hospital exactly around 10:30a to get a cup of coffee, I see this gentleman wheeling a cart with the food for the children in the hospital daycare center. I have been seeing him for the past 35 years. He looks just the same to me and I hope he feels the same although I know it's not true. As none of us can defy age. We greet each other and always try to make small conversation. Then I go to the doctor's lounge where the attendant always greets me. I know her family and she knows about mine. I feel as though there is a friend who is there to make my morning even more pleasant. If she doesn't come any day, I miss her and I would wait for her to come back so that I know that she's feeling fine. Occasionally I go to the cafeteria if I need anything special. The lady who has worked there for many years named Linda always shows up to greet me and from a distance she will shout and ask me how I am. If I take whatever I decide to take from the cafeteria she's always with me trying to help me. When I go to the checkout, the cashier greets me as well.

There is a technician whom I have known for many years. He has now become a monitor tech on one of the floors. He would often run into me in the corridors. He has the same smile for years even though after the loss of some of his hair he looks a little bit mature but to me he still looks the same He always has the same way of greeting all the doctors He always shouts from a distance "there's my doctor". It is so refreshing to see him every time.

The property manager and his staff for the building are my best friends. We have had many luncheons together. I used to invite them every thanksgiving for lunch at one of the local restaurants. I stopped doing it two years ago but did it again a year ago. I've enjoyed every minute of it. These guys are the reason that I am comfortable in this building. It is not their job to move furniture in my office, hang pictures or, make copies of the keys when we lose them. They do anything we ask for without fail. I am sometimes asked why I didn't buy my own building like many physicians did. I continued to pay rent for so many years. The main reason is my proximity to the hospital and the help provided by the property management. I would have missed out on all the adventure that goes on in this building, in the hospital, in the corridors and at the entrance to the building every morning if I was in an isolated office.

The path that led me to this journey is well paved and easy to follow. Occasionally the wind brings some pebbles to make it rough. I have learnt to walk on the rough path and keep going.

Made in the USA
Coppell, TX
03 September 2023